THE ROMANCE of REDEMPTION!

THE ROMANCE *of* REDEMPTION!

GOD BEHIND THE SEEN IN THE BOOK OF RUTH

TOMMY VINSON

XULON PRESS

Xulon Press
2301 Lucien Way #415
Maitland, FL 32751
407.339.4217
www.xulonpress.com

ISBN-13: 978-1-6628-1086-2
Ebook ISBN-13: 978-1-6628-1087-9

four years and have been married fifty-four years. I gave her six weeks to back out if she didn't want to be married to a preacher. Thankfully, she said, "yes." Like so many of my pastor friends, I married over my head. More evidence of the grace of God! To use a well-worn phrase, "I out punted my coverage." It is to my precious wife, mother of our three children, Meme to our eight grandchildren and six great grandchildren that I lovingly dedicate this book. Your encouragement and support have kept me on my feet. To paraphrase what Ruth said to Naomi, "Where I have gone, she has gone. Where I have lived, she has lived. My people have become her people, and my God is her God."

r١st. ... ... wa... . ۵. , ١. ١c ... .. 6.

redemption in the Old Testament and see how it points to Jesus in the New Testament should get this book and read it with Bible in hand. Furthermore, this book would be a welcome addition to any pastor's library. I highly recommend that you purchase it, read it, and refer to it often because you will be blessed and encouraged!

--Chuck Herring, Senior Pastor at Collierville First Baptist Church, Collierville, TN

I'm grateful for the invaluable editorial help from my friend Ken Carver

Table of Contents

PREFACE

I've been in love with my wife Rose for longer than the 54 years we've been married. But four years after our wedding I fell in love with Ruth. I was smitten. Still am. Rose knows that and is fine with it, even encourages the relationship.

Perhaps I'd better explain myself!

It was the early 1970's. Major Ian Thomas, a well-respected British evangelist, was preaching a series of messages on the Christian life at the Presbyterian church in my hometown. "The Major," as he was fondly called, taught the principles included in his classic, *The Saving Life of Christ*. The biblical basis for his messages was the book of Ruth.

I was pastoring my first church (Beulah Baptist, Myrtle, Miss.) at the time, and Gary Letchworth, the Presbyterian church's pastor, was my mentor. Gary shared with me how God had used Major Thomas to change his life and invited Rose and me to the week's services. I was eager to check out this funny sounding Brit. Never could I have imagined how that week would change my life. My love affair with Ruth, and the simple biblical principles for Christian living God revealed through her, was underway.

By now you undoubtedly understand that I was in love with the Bible's *book* of Ruth, not the woman herself!

Major Thomas taught me that the Christian life is not about *doing* my best for Jesus but *allowing* Jesus to be His best in me. The Major introduced me to a whole new way of thinking about the Christian life. How refreshing to discover that Jesus didn't call me to a life of *imitation*, but to a life of *derivation*. A mirror doesn't imitate our image when we stand in front of it, but rather derives its image from us. So, any true resemblance in our lives to Jesus Christ is not the result of our trying hard to imitate Him, but rather by our surrendering to His indwelling presence in our lives. *He* then becomes the origin of His own likeness. Spiritual fruit then becomes the natural outflow of a surrendered and abiding life. As a recovering Pharisee, I was so blessed to learn these freeing truths that helped release me from the grip of hyper-legalism.

Only a few years before, while watching Billy Graham on television as a senior in high school, I wept as hundreds of people responded to the gospel invitation. A compelling desire filled my heart to go and kneel by my bed. One thought occupied my mind—I determined to totally yield my life to Jesus

Christ. My desire from that day until this one is for Him to use me as He pleases.

Just as God used Billy Graham and that television special to bring me to my knees, God used Major Ian Thomas and the book of Ruth to show me what submission to Him—void of legalism—is like. I was blown away by how much truth our Lord packed into this small book. God introduced me to the riches of the Old Testament narrative. The principles and truths which thrilled my soul back then still do so today.

It is my sincere hope that I can unpackage some of these riches for you as we explore the spiritual adventures of Naomi, Ruth, and Boaz as they lead us on this marvelous journey of faith, grace, and redemption.

Having said all that, it shouldn't surprise you when I say that it is no accident that you picked up this book. I pray that you will be blessed, encouraged, and challenged as you read about this great "Romance of Redemption." May you learn and apply the truths cataloged in Ruth's namesake book. May she come alive to you the way she did to me fifty years ago when I first met her.

Soli Deo Gloria,

Tommy Vinson

P.S. Obviously, the choice of a key verse/passage from Ruth is somewhat subjective; but the overwhelming favorite has to be Ruth 1:16 and 17.

> *"But Ruth said, 'Do not urge me to leave you or turn back from following you; for where you go, I will go, and where you lodge, I will lodge. Your people shall be my people, and your God, my God. Where you die, I will die, and there I will be buried. Thus may the Lord do to me, and worse, if anything but death parts you and me.'"*

In my humble opinion this text marks the spiritual conversion of Ruth. In Moab she was a pagan follower of the false god Chemosh. In route to Bethlehem in Judah, she made a rock-solid commitment to Jehovah, the covenant God of the Jews. Her destiny was changed for both time and eternity. While this verse is often used in weddings, it was really spoken by a daughter-in-law who was expressing her love for and commitment to her mother-in-law. My friends, we all should frame these words into a prayer and pray them often to our Lord.

Chapter 1

When a Shortcut Becomes a Dead-End!

"Now it came about in the days when the judges governed, that there was a famine in the land. And a certain man of Bethlehem in Judah went to sojourn in the land of Moab with his wife and his two sons. The name of the man was Elimelech, and the name of his wife, Naomi; and the names of his two sons were Mahlon and Chilion, Ephrathites of Bethlehem in Judah. Now they entered the land of Moab and remained there. Then Elimelech, Naomi's husband, died; and she was left with her two sons. They took for themselves Moabite women as wives; the name of the one was Orpah and

> *the name of the other Ruth. And they*
> *lived there about ten years. Then both*
> *Mahlon and Chilion also died, and the*
> *woman was bereft of her two children*
> *and her husband"* (Ruth 1:1–5).

Greg lost his job because of downsizing. The mortgage was due. Car payments were in arrears. Insurance was unpaid. Groceries were running low. He had raked and scraped to be able to put a few thousand dollars in savings. Now he was faced with a choice. Would he use the available money to pay his bills and buy the needed groceries; or would he take the savings to the casino on a hunch that his "good luck" would be a short cut to financial success? Greg chose the casino option and quickly learned the painful, hard lesson that too often, short cuts lead to dead ends. His quick-and-easy route to financial security led him and his family to bankruptcy.

Things were not going well in Chester's marriage. He and his bride of ten years had slowly drifted apart. It seemed as if every time they tried to communicate, the effort devolved into an argument. Affection and warmth had given way to distance and coldness. Intimacy was but a memory. Chester found it easier to talk about his marriage problems with Susie at work than with his wife. After all, things were not going too great in her marriage either. She had such an understanding heart. Both of them found it was so much easier talking to one another than sorting out all the baggage that had developed over the years of their marriages. But this emotional shortcut led to another dead-end. Two broken families! Four broken hearts! Two houses filled with broken children!

Have you ever taken a shortcut that turned out to be a dead-end? I have! Just ask the mission team that I led on a disastrous tour of a remote jungle village in Central America several years ago. The previous year I had been in that village and felt I knew it well. Obviously, I didn't. Pride and a genuine desire to ensure that this team had a great mission experience caused me to bite off more than I could chew in the guide arena. After about an hour of frustrated wandering from one hut to another, all of which looked just alike to me, I laid my pride aside and asked for directions. My shortcut had become a dead-end.

In Ruth 1:1-5 we learn that Elimelech was dead-set on taking a shortcut. A severe famine plagued their hometown of Bethlehem. Bethlehem means House of Bread in the Hebrew language. The famine meant there was no bread in the House of Bread. They were immediately faced with a pressing decision. Would they do the righteous and biblical thing? Would they humbly go before their Lord in prayer, seeking His wisdom and will? Or... would they take the line of least resistance? Would they find another option even if it required them to step outside of God's will? They chose the latter!

3

Elimelech and his family decided to take what seemed at the time the easiest route. Off they went to Moab. Tragically, this shortcut turned out to be a fatal dead-end. While they intended to "sojourn" in Moab for only a short while, they ended up staying for ten years! Sin has a way of taking you further than you want to go, costing you more than you want to pay, and keeping you longer than you want to stay. That certainly happened to Elimelech and Naomi's family.

In the next few pages, we will learn the devastating price they paid to take this shortcut. That is why this chapter is titled, "When a Shortcut Becomes a Dead-End!" Short cuts are usually rougher than the main road. We learn in school that the shortest distance between two points is a straight line. I have learned by experience that we seldom take that straight route. Just as the Lord did not lead Israel in a straight route from Egypt to the land of promise, so He often allows us to take a circuitous route in order to accomplish His plan in our lives.

Now before I proceed, let me introduce a caveat here. This needs to be said: Our Lord is Lord, even of the detours and shortcuts that turn into dead-ends. They never catch Him by surprise. He never says, "Oops! What has Tommy done now?" He is able to use what we and the world would term "poor judgment calls" and "bad decisions" to ultimately pursue His divine purposes. As just mentioned, He used forty years of wilderness wanderings in the life of Israel, His chosen people. You talk about a detour! But there was much that needed to be done in them that only a wilderness experience would accomplish. Perhaps that is why the Psalmist wrote, *"It is good for me that I have been afflicted; that I might learn thy statues"* (Psalm 119:71 KJV).

In the first five verses of Ruth chapter one, I want us to look at two things:

- The Timing of God's Purpose
- The Testing of God's People

The Timing of God's Purpose: *"In the days when the judges ruled..."* (Ruth 1:1) This was tantamount to saying, "in the dark ages of Israel's experience." Morally and theologically they had reached the bottom of the barrel. Few days were gloomier in all of Israel's history. It would be like us saying, "The time of the Nazis" or "the time of the ISIS terror."

Reading the book of Judges is depressing. It involves the sevenfold repetition of the predictable cycles of sin, followed by inevitable suffering, followed by supplication for help, followed by God sending a savior in the form of a human judge. Judges is best summarized by its last verse: *"In those days there was no king in Israel: everyone did that which was right in his own eyes"* (Judges 21:25 KJV).

Idolatry, immorality, and indifference were the trinity of sins which reigned in the depraved hearts of many in Israel at that time. Their idolatry was related to their worship of the agrarian fertility gods Baal and his female counterpart Ashura. This worship led to immorality associated with lewd fertility rites. These practices were common when the events in Ruth's day were happening. Harvest time had a way of bringing out the best and worst in people.

Actually, the book of Ruth is like an oasis in the desert. I have a friend and former staff member who is a professional caver. He has shown me some of the most beautiful sights on the planet. They are pictures taken underground. These beautiful formations yield their beauty only when illuminated. The darkness cannot suppress the light.

Reading Ruth is like turning on a light so we can see the beautiful providential activity of our Lord during that difficult time. Exploring Ruth's precious four chapters is like finding a beautiful diamond in a garbage can. These eighty-five verses are like a window which allows us to look into one family's experience of faith, grace, and redemption. Interestingly, sixty-five of these verses consist of dialogue. We can eavesdrop on the family, even in these worst of times, and get firsthand information from the participants. We learn how God still has His people who will serve and love Him even though they may not understand or like the way He is governing their lives.

The Testing of God's People: *"... there was a famine in the land..."* (Ruth 1:1) There are thirteen recorded times of famine in the Bible. These times of scarcity were consistent evidence of God's judgment upon the land. If you study the book of Judges, you'll find that it isn't hard to discern the sins God was dealing with: immorality, idolatry, and indifference. These sins could easily pass as the pet sins of our own nation. They go under different names, but the disguises cannot hide their inevitable consequences.

- Immorality is now disguised as simply pursuing that which "feels good." After all, "if it feels good, do it" is today's mantra. Contemporary American idols are not cast in stone and wood but are more likely to be fashioned out of fiberglass or titanium.
- Idolatry, said A. W. Tozer, a Christian pastor and author, is "the entertainment of wrong thoughts about God." 1. (Tozer, The Knowledge of the Holy, p.1) It's the best definition of idolatry I've ever read.
- Indifference is seen in the way that even those who name the name of Christ saturate the church with their absence.

Now do you see how relevant this little four-chapter book of Ruth is for our culture and for our churches? Its relevance will become even more evident as we move further into the book.

Chapter 2

Failing the Test

I t would be wrong to assume that God sent the famine exclusively to punish His people. Famines are also allowed as tests of discipline. Someone has well said that every test is meant to produce a testimony. When God's people respond to various trials with humble repentance and teachable spirits, then God turns that punishment into discipline. His overriding desire is not to hurt us but to help us move forward in our spiritual growth. Always His ultimate goal in whatever circumstances He allows us to walk through is to help us become more like His Son Jesus Christ. (Romans 8:29)

In these opening verses we witness Elimelech facing a test. His response is an insight into his soul. Would he seek God for insight and wisdom to discover the reason for His discipline? Would he take the line of least resistance and run away from the problem? God has consistently revealed in the

Bible that His will is for us to run to Him, not from Him, when discipline comes. Later in the book we will discover that most of the people in Bethlehem chose not to run, but rather to stay, trusting God in the famine. Peter Lord was the first I heard say, "If you want to know what a man is filled with, just see what spills out when he is jostled really hard." (Sign in hallway of Mid-America Baptist Theological Seminary, Memphis, TN) I might alter that slightly and say, "If you want to see a man's heart, just watch the way he responds when trouble comes." We are about to see Elimelech's heart, and I must say it does not look too good.

One of the most helpful New Testament passages for guiding our response to God's discipline is found in Hebrews 12:4–9.

> "In your struggle against sin you have not yet resisted to the point of shedding your blood. And have you forgotten the exhortation that addresses you as sons?
>
> 'My son, do not regard lightly the discipline of the Lord, nor be weary when reproved by him. For the Lord disciplines the one he loves,

> *and chastises every son whom he receives.'*
>
> *It is for discipline that you have to endure. God is treating you as sons. For what son is there whom his father does not discipline? If you are left without discipline, in which all have participated, then you are illegitimate children and not sons. Besides this, we have had earthly fathers who disciplined us and we respected them. Shall we not much more be subject to the Father of spirits and live?"* (ESV)

The Jewish Christians to whom this letter was written were facing many tests of their faith. For example, Orthodox Jews worshipped in the ornate Temple in Jerusalem, while Jewish believers in Christ were relegated to caves and secret places. These Hebrew Christians were tempted to ask, "Is it worth it? Maybe we should just go back to our Jewish roots." Thankfully, they did not do that. Instead they moved forward in their faith. They accepted the fact that they were in a spiritual marathon, not a spiritual hundred-yard dash (Hebrews 12:1–2). They were in it for the long haul. It would require patience and endurance. In their perseverance they became our example. If only Elimelech and Ruth had access to this Scripture to read and heed. But... at least they did have the Pentateuch, the first five books of the Old Testament, and that should have been sufficient.

These verses challenge us not to ignore the test when it comes. The ESV says, "*Do not regard lightly the discipline of the Lord*" (Hebrews 12:5). The idea is that every test is to be taken seriously. Our Lord is not playing games. We are to pay attention—listen up! Jesus often said, "*He that hath ears let him hear.*" We are responsible for what we hear, but we are also responsible for what we would have heard if we had listened. Elimelech should not have ignored this test. He should have inquired of the Lord as to the cause of the famine. An appropriate response would have been for him to question whether there was anything in his or his family's life that needed to be changed and conformed to God's will. A good prayer for him would have been King David's prayer: "*Search me, O God, and know my heart; Try me and know my anxious thoughts; And see if there be any hurtful way in me, And lead me in the everlasting way*" (Psalm 139:23–24).

On the other side of the coin, Hebrews 12:5 also warns us against fainting when we undergo one of God's tests. J.B. Phillips, the English Bible scholar and translator, renders the warning in verse five as "*don't be discouraged*" when you are rebuked by Him. Ignoring a test means we don't take it seriously enough. Fainting at the test means we allow the enemy to get the victory. Satan is a sly character. If he can't get you through one door, he will try another. That is why Peter later wrote: *"Be sober, be vigilant, because your adversary the devil walks about seeking whom he may devour."* (1 Peter 5:8)

Naomi is a good example of someone who "fainted." She became weary, discouraged, and bitter as a result of failing God's test. When she arrived back in Bethlehem, she even suggested to the ladies who met her that her name be changed from Naomi to Mara. This Hebrew word for "bitter" was an apt description of Naomi at that time in her life. (Ruth 1:20) The late J. Vernon McGee, pastor, Bible teacher, and radio minister, suggested humorously that her name was changed from "Merry Sunshine" to "Grouchy Gus." (McGee, Ruth, p.14)

Hebrews 12:4–9 also teaches us that we are to rejoice at the truth revealed by the discipline. What truth would that be? That you really are a child of God. Discipline is an indication of sonship. J. B. Phillips in his Bible translation was right: *"No true son ever grows up uncorrected by his father"* (Hebrews12:7). We should be worried when we are not disciplined, rather than complain when we are. God loves us greatly, but His love is a "tough love" that does not allow us to sin imputatively.

Elimelech and Naomi discovered that their shortcut ended up as a dead-end. We will too! Sooner or later every believer will learn this truth. When we try to ignore or circumvent God's discipline, we always end up as losers.

So what is the proper response to God's discipline? One Sunday my young grandson grew restless in a rather lengthy church service. He was overhead to say, "I guess we'll just have to endure it." The ESV agrees with my grandson. It suggests that God's discipline needs to be endured. After all, endurance is one of the most authentic indications of genuine faith. I don't know the originator of this well-used statement, but it needs a new introduction into the contemporary Christian scene: "A faith that fizzles was faulty from the first."

Jesus taught His disciples that, "*You did not choose Me, but I chose you and appointed you that you should go and bear fruit and that your fruit should abide...*" (John 15:16 ESV). Fruit that abides! Sometimes the only way to tell the false believer from the true one is TIME. John later wrote concerning some teachers who had failed the test of discipline: "*They went out from us, but they were not really of us; for if they had been of us, they would have remained with us; but they went out, so that it would be shown that they all are not of us*" (1 John 2:19 NASB).

As we will see later, that was the only way you could tell the difference between Orpah and Ruth. Both made outward professions of faith in the God of Israel. Time revealed that Orpah's faith was spurious. She immediately responded to the invitation to go to Bethlehem with Naomi with emotional fervor, but soon the emotion left and so did her commitment. No abiding! No endurance! No perseverance! Sadly, this happens way too often today.

Consistently in Scripture trouble awaited those who responded to a test by forsaking the land which God had given them. Dr. Adrian Rodgers, pastor, author, and three-time president of the Southern Baptist Convention, used to say that they ended up at either dead-ends, dry holes, or detours. (Sermon, Dead ends, Dry holes, and Detours preached at Bellevue Baptist Church, Memphis, TN) We see this when Abram left the land God had given him and went to Egypt to avoid a famine. The pattern is repeated in I Samuel 27 when David, God's chosen successor to the throne of Israel, became a fugitive from King Saul, left the land and brought himself and his six hundred faithful warriors under God's judgment.

In Luke 15 Jesus told the story of the prodigal son. A young man who took a shortcut, left the land and his father's house and his inheritance. He ended up in a dead-end in the form of a hog pen. Solomon was right, *"There is a way which seemeth right unto a man, but the end thereof are the ways of death"* (Proverbs 14:12 KJV).

When problems come to God's children and they run from Him, they are rewarded for their running with a larger set of problems. Unconfronted problems have a way of growing. Ron Dunn, itinerate Bible teacher and my favorite preacher used to say, "You never fail one of God's tests—you just keep taking it until you pass it." (Dunn, Sermon) Elimelech's reward for running from God's discipline was to die in Moab along with his sons, leaving his widowed wife and daughters-in-law in dire straits.

It was bad enough to die under such tragic conditions. But to die in Moab exacerbated the situation. Psalm 108:9 calls Moab, *"My washpot"* (NKJV). A washpot is a place where dirt and filth are removed. God has such a place of discipline where He can cleanse us from sin. He sifts us and causes us to leave our "dirt" in Moab. Vernon McGee calls Moab "God's garbage can." (McGee, The Book of Ruth, p.13) It is so sad to see Elimilech and his family of believers who once lived in "the house of bread" (Bethlehem) now residents of "God's garbage can." They traded a famine for funerals—not one, but three. Elimelech died! Mahlon died! Chilion died! See what I mean? When we ignore problems—they grow!

They didn't leave Bethlehem because Moab looked so good, but because Bethlehem was so barren. How sad! In fact Moab was the last place you would expect a believing Jewish family to go. It was a cursed land, and that curse was well deserved. The Moabite people were the unhappy product of the incestuous relationship between Lot and his daughter. (Genesis 19:37) In fact God had forbidden the Moabites from any social or religious interaction with Israel. No Moabite could enter the covenant community for ten generations. Why? Because the Moabites had dealt badly with the Israelites as they traveled in their wilderness wanderings, not allowing the Jewish people to cross Moabite territory. (Deuteronomy 23:3) Under the leadership of their portly King Eglon, the Moabites held Israel captive for eighteen years during the time of the Judges. (Judges 3:14) Elimelech's family left the house of bread to eat out of the enemy's garbage can, because there was no bread in the house of bread.

Tragically, that is why some people leave the church today. It is not because the world has offered so much, but because the church is offering so little. Jesus alluded to this condition when He hinted that there are few things sadder than going someplace to find spiritual bread and all you find is a spiritual stone. (Matthew 7:9) Sometimes I feel like the little boy who inquired of his granddaddy what the plaque on the wall of the church was about. "That is a list of all the men and women who have died in the service," the grandfather replied. "Oh," said the little boy, "the morning or the evening service?"

Chapter 3

Behind the Seen!

Supposedly Mrs. Albert Einstein was asked by a reporter if she understood the theory of relativity. She is said to have responded, "Not at all, but I understand Albert, and he can be trusted."

It is fairly obvious that Elimelech's family does not understand all that God is allowing in their lives. In only five verses we have encountered famines, funerals, and failures! Adversity keeps coming like a tsunami. It looked like such a good option at the time... Go down to Moab and make a little money until the famine passes. Let the boys get a little multicultural experience. "It will be good for them," they may have thought. But the move to Moab didn't work out like they'd hoped. I'm sure the word "why?" was often heard in the Elimilech household during those days.

Unlike Mrs. Einstein's confidence in her husband, Naomi did not appear to share that same conviction about Yahweh, the God of Israel. Trouble has a way of making us bitter or better. Initially, Naomi seemed to be leaning toward the bitter option. Don't be too hard on her. After all, she has lost her husband and both of her sons in a fairly short period of time.

Likewise, you may not understand all that He is allowing in your life at the present time. Let me assure you and encourage you—He can be trusted! But before you can really embrace that truth, you must recognize that He is not only the God of the miraculous, but also of the mundane. To use an event out of the life of the prophet Elijah (1 Kings 19:12 KJV), He not only speaks through the earthquake and the fire, but also through the "still small voice." Hearing God's still, small voice requires our giving it our best attention. To hear it we must keep alert hearts in order to see how He is speaking through the circumstances of our lives, both good and bad. Elimelech's family just was not listening.

This behind-the-**scene**s activity of God is called "providence." It is also "behind the seen" for often the activity of God may not immediately and obviously be seen. The Easton Bible Dictionary defines providence as, "God preserving and governing all things by means of secondary causes." (Easton Bible Dictionary) Likewise, the Bible says, *"The steps of a good man are ordered by the Lord"* (Psalm 37:23 KJV). But notice—it doesn't say the person will always be conscious of it. I love the title of Luter and Davis' commentary on Ruth titled *God Behind the Seen.* (Luter and Davis, *God Behind the Seen,*)

As we noted in the opening pages, Elimelech's family faced death, sorrow, dashed hopes, disappointment, and infertility in Moab. Murphy's Law seemed to be at work in this situation. If anything could go wrong, it did go wrong! *"But God!"* Don't you like those two words? But God was in the midst of all these things working out His good pleasure.

The apostle Paul later was to express this truth in this familiar New Testament passage: *"And we know that all things work together for good to them that love God, to them who are the called according to His purpose"* (Romans 8:28 KJV). Don't misinterpret this verse to say that everything that happens to believers is good. Rather, hear Paul say that God is orchestrating for a good purpose all the circumstances and events that He allows to come into our lives. Paul tells us in the very next verse what that purpose is. *"For whom He did foreknow, He also did predestinate to be conformed to the image of his Son..."* (Romans 8:29 KJV). Here is Vinson's paraphrase of those two verses: "Anything that makes us more like Jesus is good from God's perspective." That interpretation requires faith in the overruling providence of God.

To the sensitive observer, God's providence can be discovered in numerous places in the book of Ruth and in one's own life. For example, we can see

God's activity **In the Trials We Face**. If we look in faith, we can see that "Behind a frowning providence, He hides a smiling face," as William Cowper wrote in his famous hymn "God Moves in a Mysterious Way." Barbara Fairchild sang a popular song titled "He Was There All the Time." It concludes, "Oh what I missed, He's been waiting right there all the time." Just because we don't see Him, hear Him, or feel Him doesn't mean He isn't present. He is the **unseen** influence behind every **scene** of every trial we face. *"Before I was afflicted I went astray, but now I keep Your word. ... It is good for me that I was afflicted, that I may learn your statutes"* (Psalm 119:67, 71).

Like a scalpel in the hands of a skillful surgeon, He wounds to heal; He cuts to cure; He hurts to help. Every test He allows is designed to bring about a testimony of His faithfulness and wisdom. That's why James, our Lord's half-brother, wrote:

> *"Consider it all joy, my brethren, when you encounter various trials, knowing that the testing of your faith produces endurance. And let endurance have its perfect result, so that you may be perfect and complete, lacking in nothing. But if any of you lacks wisdom, let him ask of God, who gives to all generously and without reproach, and it will be given to him"* (James 1:2–5).

Providence also enters our lives **Through the Various People We Meet**. God has used dear friends as well as rank strangers to influence the direction of my life. Ruth and Orpah were greatly influenced by the Elimelech family. As a result of meeting Mahlon, Ruth became acquainted with this Hebrew family. It changed the entire course of her life. Who would have ever dreamed that she, an idol worshipping, pagan Moabite, would find herself the grandmother of David, the greatest king in Israel's history? Even more, who in a million years would have predicted that she would end up in the Jewish Messiah's genealogy?

There is a lot of wisdom in the statement, "Be kind to everyone you meet. They may be your boss someday." Likewise, be kind to everyone whom the Lord sends into the normal traffic pattern of your life because He may have exciting plans for how they will impact you. Sometimes what appears to be a random meeting turns out to be a game changer.

Case in point...I was attending the Southern Baptist Convention in 2005 as a messenger from FBC Winter Park, Florida, where I was serving as senior pastor. Rose and I loved Florida. We loved Winter Park. We loved our church—but—a "chance meeting" with Dr. Chuck Herring in the hallway of the convention center was destined to change my future.

Chuck Herring was a dear friend and former prayer partner. He was just getting settled in as senior pastor of FBC Collierville, Tennessee. God was blessing. Chuck was preaching three times every Sunday morning, once on Sunday evening, leading a Bible study on Wednesday night, and moderating Men's Fraternity at 6:30 every Thursday morning. Without a doubt, his plate was full. Our conversation in that hallway centered on his need for help in the areas of preaching and teaching. The need was too critical and immediate for him to train someone right out of seminary.

The more Chuck described what he wanted, the more my own heart warmed to what he was describing. I committed to pray with him about the need. As I turned to walk away, I somewhat jokingly said, "That is a position that really intrigues me."

Needless to say I was rather surprised when, the next week, I received a long-distance call from Chuck inquiring if I was serious about what I'd said concerning the position. Leaving Florida and our beloved church family, changing churches and especially moving out of the senior pastor role was not on my radar at that time. Forty-year veteran pastors just didn't do that.

Long story short, in a matter of a few months Rose and I moved to Collierville, and I became the Senior Associate Pastor of Preaching and Pastoral Ministry at FBC Collierville. All this happened after a "chance meeting" in the hallway of the Southern Baptist Convention. God had prepared me for that moment way back in the 1960's while I was stationed in the Far East with the United States Air Force. That is when He led me to choose as my life verse, *"Trust in the Lord with all thine heart, and lean not unto thine own understanding. In all thy ways acknowledge him, and he shall direct thy paths"* (Proverbs 3:5–6 KJV).

Another indication of providence is found **In the Desires Which Occupy Our Hearts**. We see Ruth's desires expressed powerfully in one of the most beautiful verses in the entire bible:

> *"Entreat me not to leave thee, or to return from following after thee: for whither thou goest, I will go; and where thou lodgest, I will lodge: thy people shall be my people, and thy God my God: Where thou diest, will I die,"* (Ruth 1:16–17 KJV).

The Bible teaches that if we *"delight ourselves in the Lord, He gives us the desires of our hearts"* (Psalm 37:4). My own salvation experience is linked to Psalm 37:4, something I alluded to in this book's preface. Please indulge me as I broaden that story...

I remember watching Billy Graham late one night on a small black and white television as a senior in high school. Everyone else in my family had gone to bed. Graham ended his message and extended the

THE ROMANCE OF REDEMPTION!

invitation. I watched as many gave their hearts to Christ. Increasingly I felt a strong desire to kneel at my bedside and totally surrender my life to Jesus Christ. I didn't know what to say or how to say it, but the essence of what happened was that I yielded my heart to Jesus for Him to do with as He pleased. Where did that desire come from? Not from my flesh, that's for sure! God was at work, providentially moving in my mind, my emotions, and my will *"to will and to work for His good pleasure"* (Philippians 2:13).

Because action follows desire, we may rightfully expect God's providence to be seen **In the Decisions We Make**. Ruth had come to the point where she wanted her desires to reflect Naomi's desires. After she and Naomi arrived in Bethlehem, she left their house one morning not knowing where she was going to glean that day.

Easton's Bible Dictionary explains the concept of gleaning this way: "The corners of fields were not to be reaped, and the sheaf accidentally left behind was not to be fetched away, according to the Law of Moses. They were to be left for the poor to glean." Then we read these seemly benign words, *"... and she happened to come to the portion of the field belonging to Boaz, who was of the family of Elimelech"* (Ruth 2:3). But these words are far from benign. This powerful sentence gives evidence to what Luter and Davis call in the subtitle of their book, *"God Beyond the Seen."* (Luter and Davis, title page) Literally the

Hebrew says, *"She chanced upon chance."* Guess what? Our Lord is also the Lord of chance! Chance doesn't stand a chance in the presence of God.

Another beautiful example of providence is how God guided the servant who was looking for a wife for Isaac. The Bible quotes the servant as saying, *"The Lord has guided me in the way to the house of my master's brothers"* (Genesis 24:27). I love the way the old King James puts it: "I being in the way, the Lord led me." Unconsciously, without a lot of fanfare, God was at the steering wheel of this servant's life. The psalmist understood this truth when he wrote, *"The steps of a man are established by the Lord, and He delights in his way"* (Psalm 37:23).

I think of a decision my parents made to move to another county when I was a junior in high school. They felt no divine compulsion in the move. In fact, it was purely an economic choice, as my dad was offered a job in a neighboring town. I resisted the move. I did not want to leave my friends. But—had they not made that move, in all probability I would never have met my best friend and the love of my life. Now my wife of 54 years as I write this, Rose was a beautiful little black-haired sophomore when we met in the gym at East Union High School. We started dating at fifteen but didn't get serious until sixteen! We married at nineteen. I like to tell people we would have married sooner, but we were afraid to stay by ourselves at night!

I have learned to welcome and embrace the providential hand of God. I may not like what He does or how He does it, but I have learned that He always has my best interest at heart. May we all reach the point where we want our desires to reflect the desires of our Lord Jesus Christ.

We can expect Providence to actively work **In the Way People Respond to Us**. We shall see in the next couple of chapters how Ruth was naive as to how Boaz would respond to her. She was powerless to effect change on this wealthy bachelor solely by the strength of her will, the power of her intellect, or the force of her personality. But wonder of wonders! Her unseen God was working behind the scenes. He was moving on Boaz's heart and Ruth's heart at the same time. Later we'll see how interesting it is that Boaz said "yes" to the opportunity to become Ruth's kinsman redeemer, while the closer kinsman said "no." God was unseen behind the scene, influencing both decisions.

William Cowper captured this truth about God in his hymn, *God Moves in a Mysterious Way.*

God moves in a mysterious way
His wonders to perform;
He plants His footsteps in the sea,
and rides upon the storm.
Deep in unfathomable mines
Of never-failing skill

28

He treasures up His bright designs,
And works His sovereign will.
Ye fearful saints, fresh courage take,
The clouds ye so much dread
Are big with mercy, and shall break
In blessings on your head.
Judge not the Lord by feeble sense,
But trust Him for His grace;
Behind a frowning providence
He hides a smiling face.

Chapter 4

What Will It Take?

Have you ever noticed how people respond differently to the gospel message? Jesus prepared us for this eventuality when He gave us the parable of the soils. (Matthew 13:3–9) The "soil" of some people's hearts is hard and impenetrable. The truth of the gospel never makes a dent in their consciousness. Other people's "soil" is shallow. It invites a superficial response that is emotionally motivated but lacks depth. It makes a good initial showing, but it doesn't last long. Then there are those with crowded "soil." Their soil has so much going on that there is no room for any exclusive commitment. Maybe there is room to add the gospel to their already crowded schedule, but undivided attention—no way!

So here we have a variety of responses. Thankfully, we draw encouragement by His inclusion of the seed that fell into the good soil and brought forth fruit. The Lord knows just what kind of "soil" makes up our hearts. He is quite aware of the incentives that encourage our response to Him.

In Ruth's opening chapter, God uses an array of approaches to reach this young pagan Moabite woman. Theologians call these approaches providential "secondary causes." Nothing miraculous about any of these things. God is not suspending any laws of nature or intervening in some supernatural way. He is using the ordinary events of life as channels for accomplishing His divine will. We see at least five of these at work in Ruth's experience. These divinely designed providences lead her to Boaz, her kinsman-redeemer. Long before Ruth knew anything about Israel's God, He knew everything about her.

May I add—He knows everything about you and me, too! On one occasion in the New Testament, the disciple Philip was in the process of bringing his brother Nathaniel to meet the Lord Jesus for the first time. Listen to how John records their first encounter with Jesus:

> *"Jesus saw Nathaniel coming to Him, and said of him, 'Behold, an Israelite indeed, in whom there is no deceit!' Nathaniel said to Him, 'How do you know me?' Jesus answered and said to him, 'Before Philip called you, when you were under the fig tree, I saw you.'*

> *Nathaniel answered Him, 'Rabbi, You*
> *are the Son of God; you are the King of*
> *Israel'"* (John 1:47–49).

What He knew about Nathaniel and Ruth, He knows about you. Humbling isn't it?! But take heart. Be encouraged. He knows exactly what He needs to allow into our lives to accomplish His divine plan and purpose. Look at the things He permitted in Ruth's life.

First there is a **FAMINE**. I think I hear you asking, "How could God use something as tragic as a famine for a good purpose?" Good question. I would like to paraphrase the answer David Platt, a Southern Baptist pastor and author, gave in a sermon: "God in His sovereign design ordains sorrowful tragedy to set the stage for surprising triumph. In those moments when it may seem that God is farthest from us, He may just be laying the foundations for the greatest display of His faithfulness to us." (Platt, Ruth sermon)

We get no further than the first verse of Ruth before we are introduced to a famine. *"Now it came about in the days when the Judges governed, that there was a famine in the land"* (Ruth 1:1). Famines were fairly common occurrences among the covenant people of God. In fact some thirteen famines are recorded in the Bible, each of which had a disciplinary purpose. This should not surprise us because Moses wrote of these events years before.

> "But it shall come about, if you do not obey the LORD your God, to observe to do all His commandments and His statutes with which I charge you today, that all these curses will come upon you and overtake you... The heaven which is over your head shall be bronze, and the earth which is under you, iron. The LORD will make the rain of your land powder and dust; from heaven it shall come down on you until you are destroyed" (Deuteronomy 28:15, 23–24).

These verses corroborate the notion that famines can be the result of the correcting hand of God. The opposite is also true. He promised to send the rain and the harvest if His people would only trust and obey Him.

Sadly, Elimelech chose not to trust Him or obey Him. Rather than letting the famine motivate him to press closer to the Lord, he ran away. Rather than try to discern God's purpose in the famine, Elimelech saturated Bethlehem with his absence. This is exactly the opposite reaction our Lord desires. He wants His people to run *to* Him in humble repentance, asking for His forgiveness and restoration. He desires that we *"... humble ourselves and pray and seek His face"* (2 Chronicles 7:14).

But here is the shocker—although Elimelech and his family bear full responsibility for their sin of failing to stay and allow God to work through the situation, God used the famine to put this family in touch with Ruth. If there had been no famine, we probably would never have heard of Ruth, and as a result we would never have heard of Ruth's grandson, Israel's great King David. This powerfully illustrates how the Lord makes *"the wrath of man to praise Him."* (Psalm 76:10, author's paraphrase) The Psalmist wrote, *"It is good for me that I was afflicted, that I may learn your statutes"* (Psalm 119:71).

Now why did they run from the famine? From the text it appears that they were an upstanding part of the covenant/faith community there in Bethlehem. Remember, Bethlehem means "House of Bread." You would think that they would not give up so quickly on the "House of Bread." After all, this was a special little town, destined to become the birthplace of the Messiah (Micah 5:2). As we will note later, God was more than willing to bring bread back to the House of Bread when His people repented (Ruth 1:6). But at that moment they were living by sight, not by faith. Moab looked good to their carnal perspective. Solomon warned us that, *"There is a way which seems right to a man, but its end is the way of death"* (Proverbs 14:12).

The Bible calls Moab "God's wash pot," a place where filth is removed. Elimelech may have viewed Moab as a place of escape from the famine, but God viewed Moab as a place of cleansing from the sins of rebellion and disobedience. If Elimelech had been walking by faith, he would have perceived that Moab was a place which God had instructed the Israelites to avoid because of their extreme sinfulness. (Deuteronomy 23:3) When we start living by sight rather than by faith, we often try to run away from our sins and problems instead of trusting God to help us overcome them.

They left Bethlehem not only because they were living by sight, but also because they were living for the physical, not the spiritual. Some would say, "But they have to live." No! They don't have to live, but they do have to die. In the story of Jesus being tempted by the devil, we learn that it is better to be hungry *in* the will of God than full *out* of the will of God. Jesus did not succumb in His first temptation to put his own physical needs above the will of His Father. It was not the Father's will for Him to turn the stones into bread, but rather for Him to continue fasting. Jesus refused to be like Esau who sold His birthright for a bowl of soup.

One more factor contributed to their rapid exit from Bethlehem and their hurried trip to Moab, also known as "God's garbage can." Simply put, they ignored the source of their problem which was their own sinful hearts. Yes, the heart of the problem was the problem of the heart.

Jeremiah expressed a universal truth when he wrote: *"The heart is deceitful above all things, and desperately wicked: who can know it?"* (Jeremiah 17:9 KJV) Who can know it? NOBODY BUT GOD! Elimelech's family took their problem with them. Methodist evangelist E. Stanley Jones wrote, "Everywhere I go, I go too, and I ruin everything." (Jones, E. Stanley, *Surrender*). Ralph Waldo Emerson, essayist, lecturer, philosopher, and poet, said, "A change in geography will never overcome a flaw in character." (Emerson, Ralph Waldo, A-Z quotes from Google) The family thought in their pride that they could manage their lives better than God. The Devil's ploy dating back to the Garden of Eden is to get us to believe that he knows better how to run our lives than our Creator does.

In addition to the famine, God also used the **FAILURE** of Ruth's existing religion to motivate her. She was raised in Moab as a pagan idolater. Pastor A.W. Tozer taught me in his book *Knowledge of the Holy* that, "The essence of idolatry is the entertainment of wrong thoughts about God." (Tozer, A.W. Knowledge of the Holy) Ruth had been raised to think false and perverted thoughts about her pagan gods. Tozer startles us when he writes, "We don't worship the God Who is, we worship the God we think He is." (Tozer, Knowledge, p.6) Solomon put it this way: *"As (a man) thinketh in his heart, so is he"* (Proverbs 23:7 KJV). Ruth worshipped an impotent idol. Like Jesus said to the woman at the well, *"You worship what you do not know"* (John 4:22).

The main deity of the Moabites was a heartless demon-inspired idol named Chemosh. It doesn't take much imagination to envision the children fearing the priests of Chemosh. They were the ones who selected the babies to be offered as human sac-rifices whenever the idol needed to be appeased. This religious ritual was horrible to witness. A child would be selected, then placed on the red-hot lap of Chemosh. The idol was tilted so that the little one would roll down into its fiery belly. Slaves were assigned the task of keeping the fire burning fero-ciously. It would be easy to see how Ruth could grow weary of the uselessness and emptiness of these heathen practices. I would not be surprised if the demon-inspired violence of Chemosh worship left her longing for some spiritual reality. No doubt this insistence upon child sacrifice and the practice of child prostitution while worshiping their fertility gods became wearisome and grievous.

Perhaps you have despaired of the emptiness in your own religious experience. I have heard this statement too often: "Oh, I tried that religious thing, but it didn't work for me." Ruth may have even said the same thing. The devil always offers more in his religious show window than he delivers from the spiritual warehouse. He offers to fulfill your dreams— but ends up delivering nightmares. Perhaps your church membership has left you unfulfilled like that. So, you've walked away from that experience empty and frustrated. That's the nature of religion. The last thing I want in writing this book is to recommend a religion to you. I totally agree with Dr. Wayne Neal, my former Baptist Student Union director and mentor who is now in heaven. He used to say, "Religion is the heavenly way to go to hell."

What Ruth needed was not another religion to add to her pantheon of gods. What Ruth needed, and what I discovered that I needed as a seventeen-year-old young man, was a relationship with God. The emptiness and lack of satisfaction you feel about religion may be God at work in your life. This may very well be His work designed to drive you to a genuine experience of repentance and faith in the Lord Jesus Christ as your personal Savior. Perhaps, like Ruth, it is time to jettison your religion in favor of a relationship.

The third thing in God's arsenal designed to reach Ruth was a **FAMILY**. One day a foreign family moved to Ruth's hometown in Moab. She became interested in this family, especially in one of the sons named Mahlon. She had never met anyone like Elimelech's son and his family from Israel. They were different somehow. She could tell right off that Mahlon's parents were not too thrilled that he was interested in her. Later she came to understand why. Because the Moabites were descended from the incestuous relationship of Lot and his daughter, they were viewed as cursed people by the Israelites. They were seen as enemies, not only from their depraved beginnings, but also because of the way they had mistreated Israel during their forty-year wilderness wanderings. If this were not enough, there was also the incident when the false prophet Balaam influenced the Moabite women to seduce the Israelite men. This sin brought the judgment of God down upon the Moabites, and several thousand died as a result. (Numbers 23-26)

If this family had not moved to Moab, chances are Ruth never would have heard the truth about the God of Israel. As I noted previously, more than likely she never would have become the great-grandmother of King David or the great-great-great (27 greats in all) grandmother of the coming Messiah, Jesus Christ. Amazingly, as we have discovered, God used a **famine** to prod this **family** out of the nest in Bethlehem and motivate them to move to Moab. Even though this move was a **failure** to submit to the revealed will of God, as sovereign Lord, He was able to use it to accomplish His divine purpose. *"All things work together for good to those who love God..."* (Romans 8:28 NKJV).

The Bible says: *"Bad company corrupts good morals"* (I Corinthians 15:33). This verse reminds me of the well-known saying: "If you want to fly with the eagles, you can't run with the turkeys." However, the opposite is also true. Good companions make us better people. Ruth was providentially given the monotheistic and moral influence of this Israelite family. While they were anything but perfect, still they were far above the pagan infested Moabite culture.

Soon she began to spend time with her fiancé Mahlon, son of Elimelech and Naomi. Major Ian Thomas suggested, tongue in cheek, that she may have met him at the University of Moab. Perhaps she was a sales lady at the local market. We are not told how they met, but it doesn't take a lot of imagination to see how Naomi could easily move into the role of Ruth's mentor or teacher. No doubt Naomi had invested a lot of time into her daughters-in-law, teaching them about the God of Israel, things they would have never known were it not for this family's influence.

Do the people you hang out with make you a better person? Do they lift you up and enhance your character, or do they draw you down with them into the filth of immorality? Imagine Ruth and Orpah at Naomi's house. Picture them eating bagels, drinking goat milk, and talking about how God parted the Red Sea to deliver the Israelites from

Egypt. Imagine Naomi excitedly telling them how the Ten Commandments were given on the tablets of stone. Wouldn't you love to have heard her discussion about Passover and how manna fell from heaven? No doubt Naomi introduced them to the great characters of the Old Testament like Abraham, Isaac, Jacob, Joseph, and Moses. Sounds a lot like what Paul wrote to his young preacher friend Titus: "*Older women... encourage the young women to love their husbands, to love their children, to be sensible, pure, workers at home, kind, being subject to their own husbands, so that the word of God will not be dishonored*" (Titus 2:3–5).

Charles H. Spurgeon, the English preacher of the 19th century, observed that, "If we had older women like Naomi, we would have younger women like Ruth." (Spurgeon, sermon) Ruth's personal love for Naomi made her willing to listen when Naomi spoke. Their caring relationship motivated Ruth to want to learn from and please the one she loved. While this is not the highest or strongest motive for coming to the Lord, it is still a very real motive. Dear friend, if God has given you Christian parents, a believing spouse, or just a good and godly friend, you ought to get down on your knees and thank God for that. Imagine how it would thrill the heart of someone you love and who loves you very much if you gave your heart to Christ. It is no accident that God has put these people into the normal traffic pattern of your life.

Returning to Ruth's saga, it wasn't too long before the unwelcome messenger of Providence called Death came to visit their home. If God can use a **famine**, a **failure**, and a **family** to accomplish His will, then perhaps He can also use a **FUNERAL**. Bang! Bang! Bang! First, Ruth's father-in-law Elimelech met an untimely and premature death. Then Ruth's brother-in-law Chilion, Orpah's husband, died precociously. Surely this was enough for any family to endure. But then the unheard-of happened. Her husband Mahlon also died. This loss was heartbreaking! Add to their devastation the fact that neither Orpah nor Ruth had children. For any Hebrew family this unfortunate circumstance was the epitome of disappointment and failure. In the culture of that time, this failure to have children was considered disastrous.

Here was an obvious occasion for Ruth to vent all her frustrations to Naomi over the actions of her so-called God of love. It all seemed so random and so purposeless. But was it? When viewed from the perspective of a sovereign Lord, we have to say it was neither random nor purposeless. Poet Benjamin Malachi Franklin put it this way:

> Not until the loom is silent
> And the shuttles cease to fly,
> Shall God unroll the pattern

> And explain the reason why.
> The dark threads are as needful
> In the weaver's skillful hand,
> As the threads of gold and silver
> In the life that He has planned.

It will take some time, but before her little book is over, Ruth will understand why. Right now her life story is being woven with dark threads, but soon the threads of gold and silver will become obvious. Right now she is living life in the minor key, musically speaking; but soon she will be rejoicing in the major key of wonderful celebration. In the words of the powerful old Gaither gospel song, "Hold on my child, joy comes in the morning." She is coming to see that the God Naomi taught her about was much too loving to be unkind, too wise to make any mistakes, and too powerful to allow any of His plans to be frustrated.

Suddenly, Ruth begins to face her own mortality. As she gazed down into that freshly dug grave, she realized that even though she was young, so was her husband Mahlon. The thought that she too must face death was no doubt used providentially to lead her to the one true God. Over these years as a pastor, I have often seen people's hearts soften and become more open to the gospel at funerals than at any other time. Dear friend it is sobering to reflect on our mortality. The writer of Hebrews captured this when he wrote: *"It is appointed unto men once to die, but after this the judgement"* (Hebrews 9:27 KJV).

One final expression of God's providence toward Ruth came in the shape of a **FEAR** of separation. Ruth faced a crisis when Naomi announced she was leaving Moab and returning to Bethlehem. She loved Naomi. The thought of life without her was almost more than Ruth could endure. This development had the potential to leave Ruth as a woman without a country. She was no longer comfortable in Moab. She had lived long enough in the garbage can. The pagan gods no longer held her in their grip since she had learned about the God of Israel. Yet the prospect of life in Bethlehem as outlined by her backslidden mother-in-law was not too appealing either. Naomi did everything she could to dissuade both Orpah and Ruth from returning with her. Orpah, being the weaker of the two, capitulated, reversed her course, and returned to Moab, never to be heard from again.

Fear of separation was a powerful motivator to Ruth. She simply didn't want to ever be without Naomi. I can't help but wonder how many have been led to become Christ-followers this way. This happens sometimes during a church's observance of the Lord's Supper (Communion). Picture an unbelieving spouse not taking the Supper while their beloved and respected spouse takes it. This little parable of separation can sometimes be so strong that it moves the lost spouse to consider Christ. While it may not be the highest and most noble motive, nevertheless it is a motive that God can use. It was in the case of Ruth. Is someone you know and love on the wrong side of faith? What will it take for them to recognize their need for God? **Famines**? **Failures**? **Family**? **Funerals**? **Fears**?

What about you my friend? Are you experiencing the discipline of God right now? Have you taken a short cut that has turned into a dead end? What you do next is especially important. Elimelech would warn us not to run from God but rather run to Him. As I mentioned in chapter one, Ron Dunn taught me years ago that you never fail one of God's tests—you just keep taking it until you pass it! (Dunn, sermon) God never wastes life's experiences. His purpose for life's famines, failures, families, funerals, and fears is to inspire us to draw near to Him. What will it take for you?

Chapter 5

A Tale of Three Widows
(Part 1)

W ord arrived in Moab that the famine in Bethlehem was over. (Ruth1:6) There was bread again in the House of Bread. Sadly, the word came too late for Elimelech, Mahlon, and Chilion. Their three widows probably visited the graves of their deceased husbands once more before they started the fifty-mile walk to Bethlehem. It takes little imagination to envision their free flow of tears as they tried to comfort each other. Would this be the last time they would ever return to that cemetery?

Closure is so painful. They say time heals all wounds, but ten years had done little to erase the hurt in Naomi's heart. The loss of her two sons only compounded, perhaps even exceeded, the pain of losing her husband. Orpah and Ruth endure not only the grief of losing their spouses, but the humiliation of being childless—an almost unbearable circumstance in that culture.

It had been a long decade of tragedy and suffering as the opening verses of Ruth describe. They speak of famine, failure, and fatalities. These three widows didn't think life would turn out this way. When Naomi left Bethlehem, she supposed it wouldn't hurt anything just to go down to Moab for a brief stay. She probably assumed that they could make some money in Moab and soon get back on our feet. Her intention was simply to "sojourn" in Moab, not take up permanent residence. But three funerals later, Naomi had had her fill of Moab. The inexorable Law of the Harvest had borne fruit in her life. Paul warned the Galatian believers, *"Do not be deceived, God is not mocked; for whatever a man sows, this he will also reap"* (Galatians 6:7). The fruit of disobedience was bitter to swallow. But—finally—some good news! The rains had returned to Judah. The famine was over. The House of Bread was restocked!

Ruth chapter one is much more than a historical and literary record of the Elimelech family's journey from Moab to Bethlehem. It is a testimonial as to the options that are before us when we face difficult situations. God intends every test to lead to a testimony. We should listen closely to what these three widows teach us about reacting to adversity. Pay attention! Probably one of the three will reflect your default response when difficulty comes your way.

First, notice Naomi as she **Battled with Bitterness**!

> *"Return, my daughters! Go, for I am too old to have a husband. If I said I have hope, if I should even have a husband tonight and also bear sons, would you therefore wait until they were grown? Would you therefore refrain from marrying? No, my daughters; for it is harder for me than for you, for the hand of the Lord has gone forth against me"* (Ruth 1:12–13).

We will soon look into Orpah and Ruth's opposing responses to Naomi's advice, but for now I want to fast forward a few verses to unfold the degree of Naomi's battle with bitterness.

> *"So they both went until they came to Bethlehem. And when they had come to Bethlehem, all the city was stirred because of them, and the women said, 'Is this Naomi?' She said to them, 'Do not call me Naomi; call me Mara, for the Almighty has dealt very bitterly with me. I went out full, but the Lord has brought me back empty. Why do you call me Naomi, since the Lord has*

> *witnessed against me and the Almighty*
> *has afflicted me?'"* (Ruth 1:20–21)

Do you know anyone consumed with bitterness? The Bible warns us about the danger of embracing a bitter spirit. *"See to it that no one comes short of the grace of God; that no root of bitterness springing up causes trouble, and by it many be defiled"* (Hebrews 12:15).

Over the years as a pastor, I have seen people struggle severely because of decisions they made outside the will of God. Too often they get bitter at God for their circumstances. They frequently blame God for the situation they put themselves in. That was Naomi's attitude. She was battling with bitterness. That battle would be bad enough if it only affected Naomi, but it doesn't stop with her. It affected her friends and family as well. Bitterness defiles! It poisons the spiritual atmosphere and destroys peace. Bitterness is like acid—it can destroy its container. Like poisonous gas it destroys those who encounter it.

Despite her battle with bitterness, Naomi "arose and went" to Bethlehem. Her face was now toward the hometown she left ten years before. Each step took her closer to the House of Bread and further from the Garbage Can. That's what real repentance looks like! It refers not just to a change in feelings, but also a change in direction.

The word repent means to turn around. The way back to God always begins with repentance. When Jesus told the story of the prodigal son, he punctuated the moment when this rebellious young man decided to leave the hog pen and go home. Jesus said, *"... he came to his senses,"* (Luke 15:17). That is what happened to Naomi. She came to her senses. It simply means she stopped rationalizing her situation and took ownership of her rebellion and sin.

This truth is vividly illustrated through a story in the Old Testament (2 Kings, chapter 5) out of the life of Naaman, a captain in the army of Israel's enemy, the Arameans. This popular and powerful military leader had one fatal flaw. He was a leper! His Hebrew servant girl recommended that he go visit Elisha, the faithful prophet of Israel. Upon arrival at Elisha's house, he was told without any fanfare to go and dip himself seven times in the Jordan River. This apparent lapse of protocol made Naaman angry. He left in a huff without heeding the prophet's word. His pride was wounded. His hopes were dashed. His idea of healing certainly did not involve dipping seven times in the muddy Jordan River.

While on his way back home, Naaman's servant helped change his mind. He suggested that if the prophet had commanded some difficult task, Naaman would have done it. Naaman stopped his horse, reversed direction, and proceeded to the Jordan River. There he found healing just as Elisha had predicted. Picture mighty Captain Naaman making a one-hundred-and-eighty-degree turn. That is repentance! That is what Naomi did in our text. Her change of mind ushered in a drastic change of direction. She turned her back on Moab and headed for Bethlehem.

This change of mind and heart does not mean that she instantly conquered her struggle with bitterness. She still had much growing to do, spiritually, mentally, and emotionally. We see this bitterness raising its ugly head in a couple of significant ways. First, there is her response to her daughters-in-law when they joined her trek to Bethlehem. Her reply was more like that of a carnal believer than a mature disciple. Her first recorded words certainly do not sound like they are coming from a person walking with the Lord. We would expect her to rejoice in Ruth and Orpah's desire to follow her to Bethlehem. Not so! We can hardly believe our ears. She encourages them to return to Moab, not once, but repeatedly. Back to their country. Back to their pagan families. Back to their gods. Imagine that. We want to shout back across the years, "Naomi! You don't really mean that do you?" Listen to her:

> *"And Naomi said to her two daugh-*
> *ters-in-law, 'Go, and return each to*
> *her mother's house. May the LORD deal*
> *kindly with you, as you have dealt with*

the dead and with me. May the LORD grant that you may find rest, each in the house of her husband.' Then she kissed them, and they lifted up their voices and wept. And they said to her, 'No, but we will return with you to your people.' But Naomi said, 'Return, my daughters; why should you go with me? Have I yet sons in my womb, that they may be your husbands? Return, my daughters! Go, for I am too old to have a husband. If I said I have hope, if I should even have a husband tonight and should also bear sons, would you therefore wait until they were grown? Would you therefore refrain from marrying? No, my daughters; for it is harder for me than for you, for the hand of the LORD has gone forth against me!' And they lifted up their voices and wept again; and Orpah kissed her mother-in-law, but Ruth clung to her" (Ruth 1:8–14).

One significant life lesson we can take away from this passage is to never take advice from a bitter believer who is in rebellion against God's will. They lose their spiritual judgement, wisdom, and the ability to discern God's will. Their counsel will be purely human wisdom. Naomi's arguments for

Ruth and Orpah to return to Moab made sense only if you were thinking in purely secular terms. To the spiritual heart warmly in love with God, her advice was horrible. To her carnal, frustrated, rebellious heart, it just felt right for them to return to Moab. Her battle with bitterness caused her to think logically but come to the wrong conclusion.

Why did Naomi not want them to go to Bethlehem with her? The reason is really not too difficult to discern. It is alarming to what extent people, even people of faith, will go to in trying to cover their sin. Naomi didn't want to take them with her because they would be living proof to the townspeople that she and Elimelech were disobedient to God's law. They had permitted their sons to marry outside the covenant nation. To make matters worse, they had embraced cursed Moabites as their daughters-in-law. If she returned alone, no one would have to know they had broken the Law of Moses.

Naomi's battle with bitterness is also seen in her response to the women in Bethlehem once she and Ruth arrived. Listen again to how Ruth's chronicler expresses it:

> "*So they both went until they came to Bethlehem. And when they had come to Bethlehem, all the city was stirred because of them, and the women said, 'Is this Naomi?' She said to them, 'Do*

> *not call me Naomi; call me Mara, for the Almighty has dealt very bitterly with me. I went out full, but the LORD has brought me back empty. Why do you call me Naomi, since the LORD has witnessed against me and the Almighty has afflicted me?"* (Ruth 1:19–21)

Naomi could not hide the toll that her sin and rebellion had taken on both her body and her spirit. This was more than vitamins and wrinkle cream could fix! The women who met them upon their arrival inquired, *"Is this Naomi?"* Naomi means "pleasant one." She returned following a decade of sin and rebellion and told her greeters, *"Do not call me Naomi; call me Mara..."* Mara means "bitter." No wonder they asked, *"Is this Naomi?"*

Naomi's suggestion that *"the Almighty has dealt very bitterly with me"* (Ruth 1:21) betrays a jaundiced view of God's providence. It was a failed attempt to lay the blame for her battle with bitterness solely at the feet of a sovereign but apparently uncaring God. At that moment she could only see the power of God and not His compassion.

Naomi was blaming God for the condition in which she found herself, just like many people I have observed throughout my ministry. Never mind that their struggles are the result of decisions made outside of God's will. The pitiful protest against God's unfairness rings hollow. Naomi will learn a little later that God is not only sovereign; He is also loving and compassionate. He is too wise to make a mistake. He is too loving to be cruel. She will joyfully discover this truth, so let's be patient with her.

While Naomi battled with bitterness, Orpah **Struggled with Commitment**!

> "'May the LORD grant that you may find rest, each in the house of her husband.' Then she kissed them, and they lifted up their voices and wept. And they said to her, 'No, but we will return with you to your people.'... And they lifted up their voices and wept again; and Orpah kissed her mother-in-law, but Ruth clung to her. Then she said, 'Behold, your sister-in-law has gone back to her people and to her gods; return after your sister-in-law'" (Ruth 1:9–10, 14–15).

Orpah gave every impression that she loved Naomi and desired to go to Bethlehem with her. She kissed Naomi. Her emotions were stirred. Her eyes were toward Bethlehem, but her heart was still in Moab. The farther they got from Moab, the more she longed to go back. I can picture Ruth and Naomi engaging in animated conversation about Israel's

God, while Orpah fell further behind. Occasionally they may have stopped to encourage her and allow her to catch up. Sadly, she finally turned away from them and went back to "the garbage can," never to be heard from again.

The Apostle John spoke of this kind of response when he wrote, *"They went out from us, but they were not really of us; for if they had been of us, they would have remained with us"* (1 John 2:19). How can you tell if a person is genuine in their commitment to Christ? TIME! Orpah represents those who are moved emotionally toward Christ, but they refuse to commit their lives and eternal destinies to Him.

Major Ian Thomas used to say that Orpah had an awakened soul, but not a regenerate spirit. She was like the pig the apostle Peter spoke about: *"For it would be better for them not to have known the way of righteousness, than having known it, to turn from the holy commandment handed on to them. It has happened to them according to the true proverb, 'A dog returns to his own vomit,' and, 'A sow, after washing, returns to wallowing in the mire'"* (2 Peter 2:21–22). (Thomas, Ruth sermon)

You can bathe a pig in the finest body wash, spray her with Chanel No. 5, dress her in the finest clothes, and put a bow in her hair. But don't be surprised if, when she gets out of the bathtub, she goes straight back to the mud hole. Why? Because that is her nature. She is acting like a pig acts. We should never be too surprised when a lost person acts like a lost person. We make choices out of our nature. Sadly, Orpah's heart was still in Moab. Her profession sounded and looked just like Ruth's profession. Had you been forced to choose the false from the true at that moment, you could not have done it. What revealed the difference? Time.

Chapter 6

A Tale of Three Widows (Part 2)

Naomi battled bitterness. Orpah struggled with commitment. But Ruth **burned bridges** in route to Bethlehem. Her profession of faith is one of the most beautiful passages in the Bible.

> *"But Ruth said, 'Entreat me not to leave thee, or to return from following after thee: for whither thou goest, I will go; and where thou lodgest, I will lodge: thy people shall be my people, and thy God, my God: Where thou diest, will I die, and there will I be buried: the Lord do so to me, and more also, if ought but death part thee and me'"* (Ruth 1:16–17 KJV).

Now that is a profession of faith worthy of emulation. Notice the four qualities of an authentic testimony.

First there is **Repentance**. *"Entreat me not to leave thee, or to return from following after thee."* The direction and momentum of her life had changed. To repent simply means to turn and go in the opposite direction. Ruth's direction from now on was away from Moab not toward it. This is our first step toward the Savior. *"Repentance toward God and faith in our Lord Jesus Christ"* (Acts 20:21). Ruth was effectively taking Moab off the back burner of her life. That is why I call her profession "burning bridges in route to Bethlehem." Repentance involves a change of mind that ushers in a change of behavior.

Secondly, an authentic profession involves **Faith**. *"Thy God (shall be) my God."* This was quite a decision. Ruth was effectively rejecting the gods of her upbringing. All of her past was against her. She grew up in an idol worshipping home where the demon god Chemosh approved and required human sacrifice. Her profession is especially remarkable since all that she knew of Naomi's God was suffering, heartache, and sorrow. Against all odds, she believed. Like Abraham, she *"staggered not at the promise of God through unbelief; but was strong in faith, giving glory to God; and being fully persuaded that, what He had promised, He was able also to perform"* (Romans 4:20–21 KJV).

Perhaps the thing that sealed this commitment was when she saw Naomi acknowledge her own sin and repent from it. After that, Ruth knew Naomi's God was not just a deity for good people, but would also receive flawed people, like herself. She did not say, *"Thy God (shall be) my God,"* because she saw a God of pleasure, or a God of prosperity, or a God of health and wealth. She did not turn to Naomi's God because Naomi constantly preached to her. She committed her life to God because she saw Naomi repent.

The third quality of an authentic testimony is **Surrender**. *"For whither thou goest, I will go; and where thou lodgest, I will lodge."* In other words Ruth became interested in whatever Naomi was interested in. She surrendered her plans and dreams to embrace Naomi's. Bethlehem became important to her because it was important to Naomi. Believers need to understand the difference between surrender and commitment. Many believers are committed to Christ in some sort of shallow, fragile way but lack an absolute surrender to Him and His will. Ruth was not just committed to Naomi; she was totally surrendered in her heart to her mother-in-law. She held nothing back. When we surrender our hearts to Him like that, we begin to love and embrace the things Jesus loves. Since He came to seek and to save the lost, so will we. He said to His disciples, *"As the Father has sent me, I also send you"* (John 20:21). By that Jesus meant that, just as

He was sent to be the truth about God the Father, so we are sent to be the truth about Jesus. This begs the question, are you living the truth? The poet Annie Johnson Flint put it this way:

Christ has no hands but our hands
To do His work today;
He has no feet but our feet
To lead men in His way;
He has no tongues but our tongues
To tell men how He died;
He has no help but our help
To bring them to His side.

We are the only Bible
The careless world will read;
We are the sinner's Gospel,
We are the scoffer's creed;
We are the Lord's last message,
Given in deed and word;
What if the type is crooked?
What if the print is blurred?

What if our hands are busy
With other work than His?
What if our feet are trodding
Where sins allurement is?
What if our lips are speaking
Of things His lips would spurn?

How can we hope to help Him
And hasten His return?

To go where Jesus goes will take us away from our stained-glass church windows and out of our air-conditioned comfort to places we would seldom go. When Jesus went to Jerusalem, He didn't go to be seen by religious leaders. He frequented the pool of Bethesda where the lame were. When He went to Jericho, He didn't meet the mayor. He went to a blind beggar named Bartimaeus. When He went to Samaria, He did not go to the Chamber of Commerce. He went to the woman at the well.

Ruth was essentially saying, I am going to trust Naomi and her God to meet my basic needs. She must have taught this concept of faith in God's provision to her descendants well, for later her great grandson, King David, wrote, *"I have been young and now I am old, yet I have not seen the righteous forsaken or his descendants begging bread"* (Psalm 37:25). As New Testament believers we hear echoes of this promise in what Paul was to later write to the Philippian believers: *"But my God shall supply all your need according to His riches in glory by Christ Jesus"* (Philippians 4:19 KJV).

Included in Ruth's testimony was also **Consecration**. *"Thy people shall be my people."* Jesus always wanted men and women to count the cost before following Him. Sadly, modern evangelism too often tries to ease people into the church before informing them of the demands of discipleship. Jesus never did that. Up front He reminded new believers that, "*If anyone wishes to come after Me, he must deny himself, and take up his cross daily and follow Me*" (Luke 9:23). He said the gospel is like the Pearl of Great Price (Matthew 12:45)—it is worth everything.

"*Thy people shall be my people*" was equivalent to saying, "nothing shall come between us." Ruth knew if she took the God of the Bible as her God, then she would have to separate herself from the pagan crowd she lived among in Moab. Failure to obey this principle has led to the downfall of multitudes of believers. Simon Peter's denial of Christ at his pre-crucifixion trial teaches us that you cannot hang out with the enemy's crowd and live a consistent life for Jesus. Paul challenged the believers in Corinth to, "*Come out from their midst and be separate,' says the Lord. 'And do not touch what is unclean*" (2 Corinthians 6:17).

Truth is that some professing believers emulate the world in almost every area of their lives. They go to church and are bored stiff until twelve noon finally rolls around. The teaching, singing, preaching, and praying hold very little interest to them. Yet the same people can camp out at ball games, invest hours in movies, spend a sizable amount of time playing video games, then remark how time flies.

What's more, these people tell me they are going to heaven and spend eternity praising the Lord with the people of God—when they never do it here! What's wrong with this picture? The worse sort of deception is self-deception. Perhaps that is why John wrote, "If we say we have no sin we deceive ourselves" (I John 1: 8).

There is a popular song by Jennifer Lamountain titled, *I Am Determined*. The words challenge me to the core.

> I am determined to be invincible
> Till He has finished His purpose in me.
> And nothing shall shake me,
> For He'll never forsake me.
> I am determined to live for the King.

The last quality of an authentic testimony mentioned in Ruth's confession is **Perseverance**. This essential quality of true faith is implied in the words, *"and there will I be buried."* Ruth was saying that not even death could separate her from Naomi. She was in it for the long haul. She had signed up for a marathon, not a hundred-yard-dash. Endurance was more important than speed. Like the writer of Hebrews was later to write, Ruth *"(laid) aside every weight and the sin which (so easily beset her, and ran) with patience the race that (was set before her)"* (Hebrews 12:1–2 KJV). Many Bible scholars feel that the besetting sin of these early Jewish believers was the sin of unbelief which caused them to want to give up and throw in the towel. Ruth stands in vivid contrast to this spirit. She was determined to finish what God had begun in her life.

Perseverance of the saints is a term that is rarely used today. The vernacular of preference is "the security of the believer", or "the preservation of the saints." Don't misunderstand me. I am not saying that we are saved by persevering, but rather that the saved persevere. Jesus said, *"I give eternal life to them, and they will never perish; and no one will snatch them out of My hand. My Father, who has given them to Me, is greater than all; and no one is able to snatch them out of the Father's hand"* (John 10:28–29).

One of the best signs of authentic salvation is the perseverance of His people. Again I quote 1 John 2:19, *"They went out from us, but they were not really of us; for if they had been of us, they would have remained with us;"* Remaining with us! That is the operative phrase. Remaining, abiding, enduring are all metaphors for this wonderful truth. As a young preacher I heard this anonymous quote which carries so much truth, "A faith that fizzles was faulty from the first."

This doesn't eliminate the possibility of temporary backsliding in our Christian walk. The difference is that true Christians can't continue to live in outright rebellion against God without being convicted. God is longsuffering. God is gracious. God is loving. But...He is also just and holy. He cannot and will not tolerate unrepented sin in the life of His children forever. He warns. He convicts. He graciously invites us back to Himself. When all those overtures are neglected and ignored, then the pristine, holy nature of God demands that our sin be punished. Paul was right. *"The wages of sin is death..."* (Romans 6:23). Either we die, or someone must die for us. Peter revealed who that someone is, *"For Christ also hath once suffered for sins, the just for the unjust, that He might bring us to God..."* (1 Peter 3:18). Oh yes, before I forget it, the other half of Romans 6:23 says, *"... BUT the gift of God is eternal life"* (emphasis mine).

Well, there you have it—a tale of three widows. Let me ask you, which of these three widows best represent you?

- Naomi, who pictures a true believer but one who is bitter and backslidden? She reaped the harvest of consequences created by her own disobedience. Rather than facing her sin, she sought to switch the blame for her bitterness to God.
- Orpah, who was an awakened soul but did not make a true commitment to Naomi's God? She made advances as though she were going to move to Bethlehem with Ruth but chose to go back to her false gods. She kissed

Naomi, but like the kiss of Judas in the garden when they came to arrest Jesus, it was a kiss of rejection.

- Ruth, who gave us such a wonderful profession of faith to emulate? She burned a lot of bridges in route to Bethlehem. Perhaps you need to do the same. Ruth took Moab off her back burner forever. Her repentance, faith, surrender, consecration, and perseverance set a high-water mark for true commitment to God. Will you make that kind of commitment?

Let this hymn by William Kirkpatrick express your heart's desire today. It's titled *Lord, I'm Coming Home.*

I've wandered far away from God,
Now I'm coming home;
The paths of sin too long I've trod,
Lord, I'm coming home.
I've wasted many precious years,
Now I'm coming home;
I now repent with bitter tears,
Lord, I'm coming home.
I've tired of sin and straying, Lord,
Now I'm coming home;
I'll trust thy love, believe thy word,
Lord, I'm coming home.

My soul is sick, my heart is sore,
  Now I'm coming home;
My strength renew, my hope restore,
  Lord I'm coming home.

Chapter 7

What a Difference a Day Makes!

April 12, 1945—war-time President Franklin Roosevelt died. Harry Truman wrote his mother, "I had hurried to the White House to see the president, and when I got there, I found out I was the president." What a difference a day makes! (Wiersbe, Warren. *Put Your Life Together,* p. 57)

November 22, 1962—Lyndon Johnson woke up that morning as vice-president under John F. Kennedy. Several hours later Kennedy was assassinated. Johnson found himself at Texas' Dallas Love Field, on board Air Force One, being sworn in as president. What a difference a day makes!

We see this phenomenon often in Scripture. One day Moses—the man God would use to deliver His people from Egyptian bondage—awoke as a shepherd on the back side of the desert but ended that day as a commissioned prophet of God. God spoke to him through a burning bush that refused to disintegrate. As a result, Moses was a changed man. What a difference a day makes!

One day an unknown lad, David—the shepherd boy destined to become Israel's greatest king—went to take food to his brothers who were fighting the Philistines. He returned a military hero riding on the shoulders of awed warriors. A strapping teenager had killed their nemesis, the giant Goliath. What a difference a day makes!

Saul of Tarsus—the zealous Jewish Pharisee— was walking one day on the Damascus road, headed to persecute Christians. He met the risen Lord Jesus through a powerful vision, and his whole life was radically changed. Even his name was later changed from Saul to Paul. What a difference a day makes!

Perhaps a little less dramatic, but nevertheless just as real, on a spring Sunday evening in 1966 I attended Blue Springs Baptist Church to hear my uncle James Welch preach. During that rather ordinary Sunday night service with maybe forty people in attendance, my future was forever altered. I entered that service with the vocational goal of being a basketball coach. I left that evening having committed my life to preach the gospel. What a difference a day makes!

I recently received a message on Facebook from Amie, the daughter of my dear friend and former associate pastor, Charles Rogers. This precious brother died two weeks after retiring—the victim of a tragic tractor accident. Amie shared with me that she used to sing a song with her dad titled *What a Difference a Day Makes.*

What a difference a day makes,
What a change in the air.
When the glorious feeling of hope
Cuts through the doubt and despair.
Though the night seems so long,
Soon the morning will break.
We'll discover, at dawn,
What a difference a day makes.

This could have been Ruth's theme song! After what happened to her in chapter three, she would never be the same. She met a man that day who made an enormous difference in her life. She went into the fields to glean as a poor widow with no prospects for the future. She had three strikes against her. She was unwanted as a Moabite, an unmarried widow with no visible means of support, and unemployed and facing a bleak future. Amazingly, before the next day dawned, she found herself employed, desired, and admired. She went from being unwanted to being the object of the special attention and affection of Boaz, the most eligible bachelor in town. What a difference a day makes!

In this chapter we will discover three ways in which Ruth's life was profoundly altered on this one momentous day.

First, she is taken from **complete poverty** to **gracious provision** (Ruth 2:1–8). Complete poverty is a phrase not too many Americans can appreciate or understand. I know I can't. I grew up in the home of a sharecropper. My parents "robbed Peter to pay Paul" at the end of each month. Dad was a small-time farmer and a night watchman most of his older adult life. But our family never missed a meal. I never had to miss school because I had no clothes to wear, even though sometimes they were hand-me-downs. (Actually, I loved hand-me-downs because my cousins, older than me, wore good quality stuff.) We always had a roof over our heads and food on our table. Compared to many we were poor but compared to the two widows in our story we were rich.

Complete poverty accurately describes the condition of Naomi and Ruth. A widow in that day with no family was about as destitute as it gets. A foreign widow like Ruth normally faced dire circumstances. No food! No friends! No future! Naomi's prospect was not much better. The words bitter, broken, and bankrupt best describe her. Her poverty was not only physical, but it also penetrated her emotional being. She had lost not only her property but also her peace. She tenaciously held onto faith in a *sovereign, almighty* God, but her bitterness damaged her faith in a *loving* God.

Ruth, like Naomi, was also in complete poverty because of her decision to move to Bethlehem with Naomi. But even though she was unwanted, unemployed, and unmarried, she would not allow bitterness to consume her, brokenness to overwhelm her, or bankruptcy to devastate her.

Gracious provision describes what happened to Ruth when she met Boaz. No doubt over the past ten years Naomi had spent many hours teaching her Moabite daughter-in-law truths from the Old Testament. Evidently Ruth had been a very good student. When she approached Naomi and requested permission to go into the barley fields and glean, she was demonstrating an awareness of several biblical principles.

Obviously she had acquainted herself with God's plan for providing food for the poor and disenfranchised. She was clearly familiar with what Moses had written in the Pentateuch. *"When you reap the harvest of your land, you shall not reap your field right up to its edge, neither shall you gather the gleanings after your harvest. And you shall not strip your vineyard bare, neither shall you gather the fallen grapes of your vineyard. You shall leave them for the poor and for the sojourner: I am the LORD your God"* (Leviticus 19:9 ESV).

The Hebrew Social Security system was called "gleaning." In this passage the Lord is saying, "this is the kind of God I am. I love the poor. I care about the disenfranchised." Material provision then becomes a spiritual matter. God is involved. The secular becomes sacred! In fact Solomon wrote one of his proverbs to highlight this principle. *"He that hath pity upon the poor lendeth unto the Lord"* (Proverbs 19:17 KJV). Jesus even taught us to pray about such things: *"Give us this day our daily bread"* (Matthew 6:11 KJV).

The very existence of this text exposes God's heart for the poor. He said to leave the margins of the field for the marginalized of society. One way of looking at gleaning is that it was the food bank of that day. The difference was in the fact that it was not a free giveaway program but rather illustrated the "will work for food" principle. Perhaps one of the best contemporary illustrations would be people picking up aluminum cans. A person certainly will not get rich doing that, but they could manage to get enough to put a meager meal on the table. Paul expanded upon this principle when he taught in 2 Thessalonians 3:10 that if a man will not work, then he is not to eat.

I assume Naomi taught Ruth about God's provision for restoring land that had been lost, either out of poverty or death. I can picture them at Naomi's house eating a bagel, drinking goat's milk, and together reading what Moses wrote in Leviticus concerning recovering lost land. *"The land shall not be sold in perpetuity, for the land is mine. For you are strangers and sojourners with me. And in all the country you possess, you shall allow redemption of the land. If your brother becomes poor and sells part of his property, then his nearest redeemer shall come and redeem what his brother has sold"* (Leviticus 25: 23–25 ESV).

Food and property would have been important to Ruth, but this next Bible text would be of vital interest to her. She could not have known at the time just how significant this principle of a kinsman redeemer would be in her life. Imagine how unaffected she may have felt when she first read God's instruction through Moses on this subject: *"If brothers dwell together, and one of them dies and has no son, the wife of the dead man shall not be married outside the family to a stranger. Her husband's brother shall go in to her and take her as his wife and perform the duty of a husband's brother to her. And the first son whom she bears shall succeed to the name of his dead brother, that his name may not be blotted out of Israel"* (Deuteronomy 25:5–6 ESV).

God providentially used these Old Testament principles to provide for Naomi and Ruth—to move them from complete poverty to gracious provision. Early in the book we are introduced to a man named Boaz. It turns out that he was related to Elimelech and as such was eligible to be a kinsman redeemer for Naomi and Ruth. There He is again "behind the seen." This circumstance allowed Boaz to cover their needs of provision, property, and an heir for the deceased. Looking ahead to Ruth chapter four gives us a glimpse of this concept which will be developed more fully later.

> *"Then Boaz said to the elders and all the people, 'You are witnesses this day that I have bought from the hand of Naomi all that belonged to Elimelech and all that belonged to Chilion and to Mahlon. Also Ruth the Moabite, the widow of Mahlon, I have bought to be my wife, to perpetuate the name of the dead in his inheritance, that the name of the dead may not be cut off from among his brothers and from the gate of his native place. You are witnesses this day.' Then all the people who were at the gate and the elders said, 'We are witnesses'"* (Ruth 4:9–10 ESV).

The second way Ruth's life was radically altered in one day was her transition from **struggling under the circumstances** to **resting under the wings of God.**

*"Then she (Ruth) fell on her face, bowing
to the ground, and said to him, 'Why
have I found favor in your eyes, that
you should take notice of me, since I am
a foreigner?' But Boaz answered her,
'All that you have done for your mother-in-law since the death of your husband has been fully told to me, and how
you left your father and mother and
your native land and came to a people
that you did not know before. The Lord
repay you for what you have done, and
a full reward be given you by the Lord,
the God of Israel, under whose wings
you have come to take refuge!' Then
she said, 'I have found favor in your
eyes, my lord, for you have comforted
me and spoken kindly to your servant,
though I am not one of your servants'"*
(Ruth 2:10–13).

This passage introduces us to a universal question and a beautiful picture.

The universal question we need to ponder is,
*"Why have I found favor in your eyes, that you should
take notice of me...?"* Ruth spoke for all of us. I too
am in awe that the God who created this world and
all that is in it, has looked on me with favor. Civilla
Martin captured this wonder when she wrote the

old gospel song, *His Eye is on the Sparrow*. The Old Testament chronicler declared: *"For **the eyes of the Lord run to and fro** throughout the whole earth, to shew himself strong in the behalf of them whose heart is perfect toward him"* (2 Chronicles 16:9 KJV, emphasis mine).

The beautiful word picture is framed in these words *"...under whose wings you have come to take refuge."* This is a familiar metaphor used by both the psalmist and Jesus Himself to describe our relationship with God. The psalmist said, *"Be merciful to me, O God, be merciful to me, for in you my soul takes refuge; in the shadow of your wings I will take refuge, till the storms of destruction pass by"* (Psalm 57:1 ESV). Why should Ruth receive mercy? Because she sought refuge in God.

I was introduced to the big five syllable word "anthropomorphic" while a student in Bible at Blue Mountain College. It simply means attributing to our God human characteristics. Isaiah tells us about God's hands and His ears. (Isaiah 59:1,2) In another place God is presented as having wings. He is pictured as a majestic eagle protecting His young. In my sanctified imagination I can see Ruth hiding under the wings of Jehovah God as He stretches His powerful, spacious, warm, welcoming, loving wings out to her.

Ruth was startled at the undeserved favor extended to her. She should have been! Grace should take our breath away! Isaac Watts must have felt that deeply when he wrote the ever-popular hymn *When I Survey the Wondrous Cross.* Multitudes have been brought to tears of joy and unashamed expressions of worship when they sang:

> Were the whole realm of nature mine,
> That were a present far too small;
> Love so amazing, so divine,
> Demands my soul, my life, my all.

She was learning an Old Testament truth that the apostle Peter would later expand upon in the New Testament. One of his major contributions to this doctrine was that grace seems to flow wherever it can find humility. When we humble ourselves before God, we can expect grace according to 1 Peter 5:5–6. Notice that I said "expect" grace, not "deserve" grace. Ruth very keenly felt her lack of merit, and deeply sensed the undeserved nature of the grace that Boaz bestowed upon her. That same realization explains why, many years later, converted slave trader John Newton would write, "Amazing Grace how sweet the sound, that saved a wretch like me. I once was lost but now am found, was blind, but now I see." (Newton, John. Song Amazing Grace)

A cursory reading of Boaz's answer to Ruth's universal question—*Why have I found favor in your eyes?*—could lead one to conclude that Boaz gave a works answer. Did he? Did Ruth find favor with Boaz because of something she did? Word had gotten around town quickly about the arrival of Naomi and Ruth. We don't know if this scene was the day after their arrival, or several days later. Somehow Boaz had already heard about Ruth's impeccable character. He was aware of how she had left family, friends, country, and even her gods to follow Naomi to Bethlehem. With those facts fresh in his mind, was he saying God showed her grace because of the way she treated her mother-in-law Naomi? Read my lips! No! He said she found grace because she fled to Jehovah and got under His protecting wings. This is a beautiful way of saying she put her trust totally in Him. (Ruth 1:16–17)

The implication of this text is that she treated her mother-in-law with kindness and love because Jehovah had treated her with kindness and love. First, her faith embraced God's grace; then it produced a gracious spirit toward Naomi. Faith does that. We are not saved by works, but by a faith that works. This was a matter of special concern for our Lord's half-brother James. He lived in the household with Jesus for years without really understanding who He was. Once he finally placed his faith in Jesus as the Christ, he became concerned about those who claimed to have faith, but their lives gave no evidence of an authentic relationship with the Lord.

Let James' challenge from the New Testament book
that bears his name challenge you.

> *"What use is it, my brethren, if someone
> says he has faith but he has no works?
> Can that faith save him? If a brother or
> sister is without clothing and in need of
> daily food, and one of you says to them,
> 'Go in peace, be warmed and be filled,'
> and yet you do not give them what is
> necessary for their body, what use is
> that? Even so faith, if it has no works,
> is dead, being by itself. But someone
> may well say, 'You have faith and I have
> works; show me your faith without the
> works, and I will show you my faith by
> my works'"* (James 2:14–18).

Paul spoke to the matter of faith and works when
he wrote to the Ephesians, *"For we are His work-
manship, created **in** Christ Jesus **for** good works..."*
(Ephesians 2:10, emphasis mine). Works follow faith
as surely as breath follows life. Titus confirmed this
truth when he wrote: *"This is a trustworthy statement; and concerning these things I want you to speak
confidently, so that those who have believed God will
be careful to engage in good deeds. These things are
good and profitable for men"* (Titus 3:8). When the
word faith is used as a noun, it refers to that body

of truth we Christians hold precious in the Bible. When used as a verb, faith refers to that attitude of trust which inevitably produces fruit in the life of the believer. Faith animates! It was true of Ruth when she—by faith—sought refuge under the wings of Jehovah. It is true of believers today when they, by faith, find forgiveness, comfort, protection, and peace under the wings of our dear Lord Jesus.

As mentioned earlier, this poignant metaphor was also used by Jesus Himself: *"O Jerusalem, Jerusalem, the city that kills the prophets and stones those who are sent to it! How often would I have gathered your children together as a hen gathers her brood under her wings, and you were not willing"* (Matthew 23:37 ESV). Respected author and pastor John Piper teaches that God is not an employer looking for employees; rather He is an eagle looking for people who will take refuge under His wings. (Piper, Ruth sermon) Taking refuge is another way of saying faith. Many times I heard Bible teacher Manley Beasley say that nothing pleases God like faith. He helped me to understand the principle that faith honors God, and God honors faith. (Beasley, Manley, Faith Notebook)

Ruth's third transition—all of which happened in that one special day—was going from **reaping hurtful consequences** to **enjoying God's kind blessings.** For ten years she and Naomi had been reaping painful consequences of lives lived outside the perfect will of God. A famine and three funerals did much to humble them, but it also positioned them for better days. They were now ready to enjoy God's kind blessings. They were about to learn what the Psalmist meant when he wrote: *"Before I was afflicted I went astray, But now I keep Your word... It is good for me that I was afflicted, that I may learn Your statutes"* (Psalm 119:67, 71).

Now they are prepared to receive the varied blessings of God. First, there was the blessing of **guidance**. *"Then Boaz said to Ruth, 'Now, listen, my daughter, do not go to glean in another field or leave this one, but keep close to my young women. Let your eyes be on the field that they are reaping, and go after them'"* (Ruth 2:8–9 ESV). These verses highlight the fact that God's guidance includes closing doors as well as opening doors. There were no markers, mailboxes, names or addresses in Bethlehem's fields. The people of Bethlehem knew where the boundaries were, but Ruth was a foreigner with no prior knowledge of the layout of the fields. But buckle your spiritual seat belt and hold on, because *"... she happened to come to the part of the field belonging to Boaz"* (Ruth 2:3 ESV).

This verse signals that **God was silently at work behind the seen directing her steps**. Don't miss that! Sometimes it is hard to see the hand of God at work through the windshield, but it begins to make much more sense as we look through the rear-view mirror. I mentioned earlier that as a young Christian

I was challenged to select a life verse. I chose, *"Trust in the Lord with all your heart, and lean not on your own understanding. In all your ways acknowledge Him, and He will direct your paths"* (Proverbs 3:5–6 NKJV). Ruth was operating not out of her understanding, but out of her trust in the Lord. In this she becomes our example in our own walk with our Lord Jesus.

Next, Boaz provided the blessing of **protection**. Ruth 2:9 reads, *"Let your eyes be on the field that they are reaping, and go after them. Have I not charged the young men not to touch you? And when you are thirsty, go to the vessels and drink what the young men have drawn."* (ESV). Ruth was young and attractive. Some of *"the young men"* would not respect her since she was a foreigner. She was vulnerable. No doubt godly Boaz was concerned that some might use the occasion to confront "the Moabite" with racial or religious insults—or worse. She was easy prey for any low minded, lust motivated young man. Harvest time, and especially threshing time, was infamous as a time of immorality. Prostitutes plied their trade more aggressively during these days of prosperity and cheerfulness. So Boaz provided those things she could not provide for herself.

Boaz was ahead of his time. Several millennia before the "Me Too" movement, he implemented the first anti-sexual-harassment policy in the business world. It went far beyond the letter of the law. Thankfully, our Greater Boaz, the Lord Jesus, has promised to protect His children. Paul wrote the Philippians that, *"God would supply all (our) needs according to His riches in glory in Christ Jesus"* (Philippians 4:19). One of those needs is the provision of protection.

My family and I experienced God's blessing of protection when we were a young family. In the early morning hours, gasping for air, one of our young sons woke me up. That's when I realized that my wife was listless and unresponsive. Our other son was experiencing violent nausea and diarrhea. It was obvious that something was terribly wrong. Turned out to be carbon monoxide poisoning! We were able to get out of the house just in time to avoid a tragedy. Our family ended up in the hospital with pneumonia. Normally, you don't wake up in that situation. Had our son not awakened gasping for air, we all probably would have died. It is my deep conviction that our Heavenly Boaz was watching over us. For years I have often quoted this verse as a prayer at night, *"In peace I will both lie down and sleep; for you alone, O lord, make me dwell in safety"* (Psalm 4:8 ESV).

In addition to guidance and protection, Boaz also provided Ruth with the blessing of **grace**. Ruth 2:10 reads, *"Then she fell on her face, bowing to the ground and said to him, 'Why have I found favor in your sight that you should take notice of me, since I am a foreigner?'"* Finding favor in Boaz's eyes was synonymous with finding grace. Grace combines the notions of desire and power. It gives us the aspiration to please God and then provides the strength to do it. Ruth found grace; consequently, she hid underneath the wings of God. Pastor John Bunyan, perhaps best known for writing *The Pilgrim's Progress*, expressed the thought like this:

> Run, John run, the Law commands,
> But gives us neither feet nor hands.
> Far better news the gospel brings,
> It bids us fly and gives us wings.
> ("thegospelcoalition.org." The origin of this
> saying is disputed. Spurgeon attributed it to
> John Berridge, others to Scottish preacher
> Ralph Erskine.)

Our Greater Boaz also has extended grace to us as His children. Paul reminded the Ephesian believers of this fact when he wrote, *"For by grace you have been saved through faith, and that not of yourselves, it is the gift of God; not as a result of works, so that no one may boast"* (Ephesians 2:8–9).

In one day Ruth went from poverty stricken to bountifully blessed. So did Naomi. When Naomi entered Bethlehem, she said that she had returned "empty." That emptiness was about to change. Guidance, protection, provision, and grace were special and unexpected gifts from Boaz. When Ruth left the house that morning, she was no doubt hoping just to get enough grain to abate their hunger for one more day. She was in for an enormous surprise. Surprise is probably an understatement. Gleaning was hard work. The return for the effort was minimal. To have an unexpected benefactor help her so graciously and generously was more than she could imagine.

Along with Ruth's many other great qualities, we must add industriousness. Here is how our narrator reveals this quality:

> "At mealtime Boaz said to her, 'Come here that you may eat of the bread and dip your piece of bread in the vinegar.' So she sat beside the reapers; and he served her roasted grain, and she ate and was satisfied, and had some left. When she rose to glean, Boaz commanded his servants, saying, 'Let her glean even among the sheaves, and do not insult her. Also you shall purposely pull out for her some grain from the bundles and leave it that she may glean, and do not rebuke her'" (Ruth 2:14–16).

The Mosaic Law required only that the harvesters not go back over the fields to pick up what was dropped. Boaz went much further than the Law demanded. He told the reapers to purposefully *"... pull out for her some grain... and leave it that she may glean"* (Ruth 2:16). That evening she took an ephah home to Naomi. An ephah's volume was equal to about six gallons and would weigh 30-50 pounds. It would feed fifty soldiers for one day. Obviously then, it would supply two widows for several weeks. In contrast the average gleaner could expect to glean one or two pounds of grain per day. Boaz also told Ruth to go to the water jars that the men had filled and get a drink whenever she got thirsty. This privilege was something the other gleaners did not have. This really is jaw-dropping, for it was normally the women who served the men, not vice versa.

Dr. Sharon Enzor, Provost and Vice President of Blue Mountain College, shared with me an article her pastor had shared in the previous Sunday's message. It highlights this aspect of our Heavenly Boaz. Moses and the people were in the desert, but what was he going to do with them? They had to be fed, and feeding between two and three million people requires a lot of food. The people needed 2,000 tons (4,000,000 pounds) of food each day. To bring that much food would require three freight trains per day, each a mile long! In the desert they needed firewood to cook and keep warm. All those nightly fires would require 4,000 tons (8,000,000 pounds) of wood and a few more freight trains, each a mile long. Of course, they needed water. If they had only enough water to drink and wash a few dishes, it would take 11 million gallons per day, not to mention a freight train with tank cars 1,800 miles long, just to bring the water. And then another thing: they had to get across the Red Sea in one night. If they went on a narrow path, double file, the line would be 800 miles long and would require 35 days to get through; so there had to be an opening in the sea three miles wide so that they could walk 5,000 abreast to get over in one night. Each time they camped, they needed a campground two-thirds the size of the state of Rhode Island, about 750 square miles. They journeyed in the desert forty years. (Summary of article referred to by Jason Howell, pastor Flat Rock Baptist Church, Blue Mountain, MS.)

Do you think Moses worked all this out before he left Egypt? Not hardly! Moses put his trust in God, and God handled things every day for 40 years. If you think God can't handle your problems, THINK AGAIN! Even back in the days of Moses God was actively at work behind the seen!

Can you identify with these widows in their broken, bankrupt, and bitter state? Are you struggling under circumstances when God really wants you to rest under His wings? Don't you think it is time to stop reaping hurtful consequences and start enjoying God's many blessings? The next chapter will give us specific help in how to access the tremendous resources of guidance, grace, protection, and provision which our Heavenly Boaz makes available.

What a difference a day makes when Jesus is involved!

Chapter 8

Getting at the Feet of Him Who has the Right to Redeem!

I've read and heard about some rather strange marriage proposals in my life. They range from popping the question on roller coasters, to hiding rings in pizzas, to running the proposal as part of the coming attractions at the theater. My grandson proposed in a hot air balloon. A young friend with close friends in the police department had them stop and execute a fake arrest of him. While they had him in handcuffs and on his knees, he looked over at his panic-stricken fiancé in the passenger side of the car and asked, "Will you marry me?" She wanted to hurt him rather than marry him at that moment! But it worked. She said "yes."

But I must say Ruth's proposal to Boaz tops them all. We find it recorded in Ruth 3, verses 1–13…

Then Naomi her mother-in-law said to her, "My daughter, shall I not seek security for you that it may be well with you? Now is not Boaz our kinsman, with whose maids you were? Behold, he winnows barley at the threshing floor tonight. Wash yourself therefore, and anoint yourself and put on your best clothes, and go down to the threshing floor; but do not make yourself known to the man until he has finished eating and drinking. It shall be when he lies down, that you shall notice the place where he lies, and you shall go and uncover his feet and lie down; then he will tell you what you shall do." She said to her, "All that you say I will do." So she went down to the threshing floor and did according to all that her moth-er-in-law had commanded her. When Boaz had eaten and drunk and his heart was merry, he went to lie down at the end of the heap of grain; and she came secretly, and uncovered his feet and lay down. It happened in the middle of the night that the man was startled and bent forward; and behold, a woman was lying at his feet. He said, "Who are you?" And she answered, "I am Ruth your maid. So spread your covering over your maid, for you are a close relative." Then he said, "May you be blessed of the Lord, my daughter. You have shown your last kindness to be better than the first by not going after young men, whether poor or rich. Now, my daughter, do not fear. I will do for you whatever you ask, for all my people in the city know that you are a woman of excellence. Now it is true I am a close relative; however, there is a relative closer than I. Remain this night, and when morning comes, if he will redeem you, good; let him redeem you. But if he does not wish to redeem you, then I will redeem you, as the Lord lives. Lie down until morning."

The good news is that Boaz has been kind, generous, and respectful to Ruth throughout the harvest season. The bad news from Naomi's perspective is that he is no closer to proposing to Ruth than he was when he first met her in the barley field. Apparently he has not gotten the subtle message. He needs something a little more overt.

Gary Phillips captured this reality in the Holman Old Testament Commentary when he wrote:

"If Naomi, Ruth's mother-in-law, were to write for advice from a second millennium B.C. advice column, it might read like this: "Dear Abigail, my widowed daughter-in-law has daily contact with an older man who shows concern about her and respect for her. In fact, from the moment he saw her, he was deeply interested and has treated her like a princess. But fast forward two months and he still has not said one word to take their relationship to the next level. She likes him, but he's not getting any younger! How do we get him to ignite his inertia, to light his lethargy, to cancel his coma? Signed, Befuddled in Bethlehem." (*Holman Ruth* p.329)

Evidently Boaz had no immediate plans to change his bachelor status. Furthermore the harvest season was ending. The opportunity for Ruth and Boaz to see each other regularly was closing fast. So out of Naomi's creative mind came a plan. She gave Ruth instructions for presenting herself as a potential spouse for Boaz. The plan was wisely designed to allow Boaz the opportunity to say "no" with minimal embarrassment—if he so chose. Under the cover of darkness, in the middle of the night, no one else would have to know.

Interestingly, some of the words Naomi used to motivate Ruth to pursue her relationship with Boaz are the same words used later in King David's declaration that the time of mourning was over for the death of his and Bathsheba's son. *"So David arose... washed, anointed himself, and changed his clothes"* (2 Samuel 12:19–20). Naomi used them to encourage Ruth that her time for mourning Mahlon's death had ended. She said to Ruth, *"Wash yourself therefore, and anoint yourself and put on your best clothes."* It was time to get on with life.

Naomi's crafty plan involved sending Ruth to the threshing floor to find and approach Boaz. She was to wait patiently until he had finished his meal and lay down to rest. After he had gone to sleep, she was to lie down at his feet.

I love the way Eugene Peterson puts it in his Bible paraphrase *The Message*:

> *"My dear daughter, isn't it about time I arranged a good home for you so you can have a happy life? And isn't Boaz our close relative, the one with whose young women you've been working? Maybe it's time to make our move. Tonight is the night of Boaz's barley*

> *harvest at the threshing floor"* (Ruth
> 3:1–2 The Message).

In response to Naomi's strategy, Ruth prepared herself for this encounter with Boaz. Hidden in these instructions is also a picture of how we can approach our Heavenly Boaz, the Lord Jesus. To start with, she was to make herself attractive by taking a good bath. Gleaning was hard, dirty work. Any young lady wanting to be near and impress her lover would want to get rid of the dirt and grime from the workday. Water was not plentiful, consequently baths were not that frequent. But this night was special. Naomi encouraged Ruth to get as clean as possible before setting out to meet her potential kinsman redeemer.

"Wash yourself!" The words are remarkably similar to what Paul told the believers in Corinth. He wrote, *"... let us cleanse ourselves of all filthiness of the flesh and spirit..."* (2 Corinthians 7:1 KJV). In other words, take responsibility for pursuing holiness. How do we do that? How do we wash ourselves? By the Word of God. When we hear, read, meditate on, memorize, and especially obey the Word of God, we are made clean. David said, *"Thy word have I hid in mine heart, that I might not sin against thee"* (Psalm 119:11 KJV). We read the Bible, but really the Bible reads us. A simple Google search reveals that the great reformed pastor John Bunyan and the

eighteenth-century evangelist Dwight L. Moody both wrote in the fly leaves of their Bibles: "This book will keep you from sin, and sin will keep you from this book."

Naomi then suggested to Ruth that she anoint herself. Vinson's paraphrase of that is, "rub on some Bouquet of Bethlehem." In other words, be nice to be near. It was common in that culture for people to use fragrant oils to protect and heal their bodies and to make themselves pleasant to others. A bride would be especially careful to wear fragrant perfume that would make her smell nice. Solomon wrote in his famous love song, *"For your love is better than wine. Your oils have a pleasing fragrance..."* (Song of Solomon 1:2–3).

Anointing oil speaks of the presence and the working of the Holy Spirit in the lives of believers. All Christ-followers have received the anointing of the Spirit. (1 John 2:20, 27) Consequently, every believer ought to be a sweet-smelling fragrance to Christ. The Apostle Paul felt this way when he wrote to the Corinthian believers, *"For we are a fragrance of Christ to God among those who are being saved and among those who are perishing; to the one an aroma from death to death, to the other an aroma from life to life"* (2 Corinthians 2:15–16). Let me ask you a question: "Do you smell like Jesus?" What does He smell like, you ask? Like fragrant fruit! The fruit of the Spirit is *"... love, joy, peace, patience, kindness,*

goodness, faithfulness, gentleness, self-control..."
(Galatians 5:22).

Naomi also told Ruth to change her clothes.
(Ruth 3:3c) She was to put off the garments of a
sorrowing widow, sometimes called widow's weeds.
Using modern jargon, she was to "dress to impress."
Like David said when his son died, it was time to get
on with life. The time of mourning was over. Time
to focus on the future, not the past. Ruth undoubtedly didn't have a large wardrobe. Remember, she
brought everything she owned with her when she
traveled by foot from Moab to Bethlehem. That being
said, she probably had one special garment for festive occasions.

In Scripture, clothing carries a spiritual
meaning. After they had sinned in the Garden of
Eden, Adam and Eve tried to cover themselves with
fig leaves. This self-effort attempt did not work.
Consequently we find them hiding from the Lord.
Hiding from Omniscience is a challenging proposi-
tion. Chronicles tells us, "...the eyes of the Lord run to
and fro throughout the whole earth..." (2 Chronicles
16:9 KJV). Sadly, they were hiding from the only One
who could adequately deal with their sin problem.
Only the Lord could forgive them and clothe them
acceptably.

In God's economy blood had to be shed in order
for them to be forgiven. Animals had to die in order
for Adam and Eve to be clothed (Genesis 3:1–8, 21).

The writer of Hebrews stated emphatically, *"without the shedding of blood, there is no forgiveness of sin"* (Hebrews 9:22). This verse declares how our heavenly Kinsman Redeemer also had to die in order for us to be clothed in His righteousness. We can't come into God's presence in our own righteousness, for, *"... all our righteousnesses are as filthy rags..."* (Isaiah 64:6 KJV). We can only come before God in the righteousness of Jesus Christ. *"For God made Him who knew no sin to be sin on our behalf, so that we might become the righteousness of God in Him* (2 Corinthians 5:21).

Jesus taught this truth in the parable of the wedding garment found in Matthew 22. The major point of this parable is that the required garment was also a provided garment. The righteousness which God requires is the righteousness which only God can provide! Every demand that He makes upon us is a demand which He makes upon Himself. Every command He gives us includes—stated or implied—a promise to provide whatever is needed to fulfill that demand.

Included in Naomi's plan was the necessity for Ruth to be focused and attentive. She was to carefully observe where Boaz's tent was located and to note exactly where he lay down. There was no room to make a mistake here. To end up in the wrong tent— well, you can imagine! There was only one who qualified to be her kinsman redeemer, and she did not want to miss him.

During this threshing season, there would have been many farmers on the threshing floor. This was a time to celebrate. Harvest time was a festive time. The grain was ready to go to market. They had worked hard, and now they could reap some reward for all their labor.

It was much that way when I was growing up in the home of a sharecropper in Mississippi. When the cotton was picked, I would get to go with Dad to the cotton gin. It was a time of joy and celebration—a momentary reprieve. The recent rigors of pulling that heavy cotton sack up a row were replaced by a time of rest and relaxation. In those days few feelings could match the joy of feeling the breeze in my face as I rode the tractor-pulled wagon to the gin.

In Ruth and Boaz's day, harvest time was also when evil could be expected to raise its ugly head. Often prostitutes would come and ply their trade during the harvest celebration. The farmers became vulnerable targets for these women while they guarded their grain all night. That is why Boaz was so startled when Ruth uncovered his feet. He was so relieved to hear her familiar voice and sense her upright and holy motives. Everything we know about the character and integrity of Ruth and Boaz removes any suspicion of inappropriate sexual behavior in this incident.

So, Ruth was to be attentive to Boaz exclusively. He was to be the focus of her heart. In other words, she was not to take her eyes off him. Similarly, we are to be solely focused on our heavenly Kinsman Redeemer. Why? Because *"... there is no other name under heaven given among men by which we must be saved"* (Acts 4:12). Helen H. Lemmel's hymn *Turn Your Eyes Upon Jesus* puts it this way:

Turn your eyes upon Jesus,
Look full in His wonderful face,
And the things of earth will grow strangely dim
In the light of His glory and grace.

Ruth needed to learn another lesson. It was not enough just to be attentive; she also had to be assertive. (Ruth 3:3–4). So far the passive approach had not worked. Boaz's nuptial inertia had not changed. He seemed inordinately conscious of their age difference. He was so uncertain of Ruth's desires that he failed to advance their relationship beyond just friendship. That's why Ruth had to take the initiative and be assertive.

According to Naomi's plan, Ruth was to place herself at the feet of her potential redeemer. This was a discreet, ethical, and appropriate way for her to express her availability. To "get at the feet" of Boaz was a sign of her full commitment to him as her redeemer. She highlighted that commitment by calling herself *"Ruth your maid."* She was assuming the place of a humble servant; and by doing so she was saying, "Boaz, I want to you to be my redeemer husband." It was unquestionably a proposal!

The actual request is framed this way: *"spread your <u>covering</u> over your maid."* The KJV uses the term <u>*skirt*</u> in place of *covering*. The ESV uses the term <u>*wings*</u>. Interestingly, all three translations (and others) use *wings* when rendering the same Hebrew word in Ruth 2:12. That's when Boaz expressed his high regard for Ruth's testimony. There, he said in effect, "she got under the wings of God." Here, she was essentially saying, "I want you to do for me physically what God has done for me spiritually. I got under His wings to be saved from my guilt and sin. Now I want to get under your wings for provision, protection, and procreation of an heir for our family."

Seeing Ruth at Boaz's feet reminds me so much of Martha's sister Mary in the New Testament. She was always placing herself at the feet of Jesus (Luke 10:39). Her love for Him created an appetite within her to learn from Him everything she could. To use the vernacular of Ruth, she too was getting at the feet of the One who had the right to redeem her. Jesus commended her for that single-minded focus. He held her up as an example to emulate.

Ruth not only had to be attractive, attentive, and assertive, but she also had to be available (Ruth 3:4–5). As we have seen, when she said, *"I am your servant,"* she was putting her entire life into Boaz's hands. Her agenda had become his agenda. Her plans gave way to his plans. In New Testament terms (Luke 9:23) she had, *"denied herself and taken up her cross daily to follow Him"*—or in Ruth's case, to follow Boaz. Hear him respond to her: *"I will do for you whatever you ask."* Sounds like a smart husband already! Boaz's desire was to not only be a hearer of the word, but also a doer. Listening is vital to any good marriage relationship, but it must not stop there. When the scripture teaches, *"Husbands, love your wives"* (Ephesians 5:25), it had more than listening in mind. Love is an action word. Not just something we feel, but something we do.

When you put an obedient servant (Ruth) with a person completely committed to obey all God says (Boaz), something exciting can happen. We will see an example of this a little later. We can't take our place at Jesus' feet without hearing and obeying His commands. In his popular song "Trading my Sorrows," Darryl Evans encourages us to say, "I'll say 'Yes, Lord, yes' to Your will and to Your way."

Chapter 9

Requirements for the Kinsman Redeemer

Naomi's plan was a good one. Basically she was telling Ruth to do what God's Word tells us to do, *"Get at the feet of Him who has the right to redeem."* The right to redeem! Exactly what does that mean? The statement implies that not everyone has that right. It quickly becomes obvious that this plan required a most special person for its implementation. That person was called a kinsman redeemer. There were **three prerequisites** to be met before anyone could fill this role.

First and preeminently, he must have been **closely related** to the person who needed redemption. We are not told what the relation was between Elimelech and Boaz, but ideally (though not exclusively) the kinsman redeemer was to be a brother of the deceased. With the limited information we are given in the book it is hard to be dogmatic about the exact nature of their relationship. But one thing is sure...they were related. Without this fact being true he could not have been a potential kinsman redeemer.

Before Jesus could be our Redeemer, He had to become one of us. This prerequisite injects great purpose and meaning into the doctrine of Jesus' virgin birth and incarnation. It was not incidental nor window dressing to a great life. It was vital to His role as redeemer. This prophesied event (Isaiah 7:14 and 9:6) allowed our Lord to be fully God and fully man, but without a sin nature. He completely fulfilled this requirement for being our Kinsman Redeemer. Therefore, He was able to perfectly understand our humanity. He knows full well that we are but dust (PS 103:14). Being fully man allowed Him to be *"... tempted in all things as we are."* Being fully God allowed Him to be, *"... yet without sin"* (Hebrews 4:15).

> The writer of Hebrews highlighted this point when he wrote: *"Inasmuch then as the children have partaken of flesh and blood, He Himself likewise shared in the same, that through death He might destroy him who had the power of death, that is, the devil... Therefore, in all things He had to be made like His brethren, that He might be a merciful and faithful High Priest*

*in things pertaining to God, to make
propitiation for the sins of the people.
For in that He Himself has suffered,
being tempted, He is able to aid those
who are tempted"* (Hebrews 2:14,
17–18 NKJV).

Second, a near kinsman needed to have **adequate resources** to take on the responsibility of redeeming. It was imperative that he be financially able not only to purchase the property, but also to take care of the widow. Redemption may be free to the one being redeemed, but it is not cheap. Redemption comes at a high price, whether physical or spiritual. To its recipients it is a gift. But someone has to pay for that gift. To the one who provides redemption, it is extremely costly. Our Heavenly Boaz paid the ultimate price of His life in order for us to be redeemed. *"In whom we have redemption through His blood, the forgiveness of sins..."* (Ephesians 1:7 KJV).

Boaz is presented as *"... a man of great wealth"* (Ruth 2:1). This term can refer to the richness of his character as well as his financial prosperity. In this case it probably refers to both. His ownership of the barley field in Bethlehem confirms his substantial financial resources. His gracious, generous and benevolent spirit proves his abundant resources of character and integrity. It didn't matter how much

Boaz wanted to redeem his family member, if he could not afford it, he could not do it.

We have not yet exhausted these prerequisites. It was not enough to be a relative. It was not enough to have adequate resources. There was a third...

The redeemer must also have **resolve**. He had to be **willing to redeem**. Thankfully, our Heavenly Boaz—Jesus Christ—has proven that He is not only related and resourceful, but He is also resolved and willing to be our Kinsman Redeemer. Peter highlights this wonderful truth in his second epistle, *"(He is) not willing that any should perish, but that all should come to repentance"* (2 Peter 3:9 KJV).

Was Boaz willing to be Ruth's kinsman redeemer? Was he resolved? So far he had not played his hand. His actions toward Ruth were benevolent and generous, but any willingness to act as her kinsman redeemer had been kept secret. We know Boaz was **related** to Naomi's husband Elimelech and therefore to Elimelech's son Mahlon, Ruth's husband. We know he had **adequate resources** and was able to redeem. Our biggest question mark concerns this third characteristic. We need to know... Boaz, are you **willing**? Do you have the **resolve** to redeem Ruth? We are about to find out.

Naomi's plan was ready to be implemented. Now comes Ruth's proposal.

> *"So she went down to the threshing floor
> and did according to all that her moth-
> er-in-law had commanded her. When
> Boaz had eaten and drunk and his
> heart was merry, he went to lie down
> at the end of the heap of grain; and
> she came secretly, and uncovered his
> feet and lay down. It happened in the
> middle of the night that the man was
> startled and bent forward; and behold,
> a woman was lying at his feet. He said,
> 'Who are you?' And she answered, 'I
> am Ruth your maid. So spread your
> covering over your maid, for you are a
> close* relative'"* (Ruth 3:6–9).

This proposal involves quite a powerful meta-phor. Listen to Ruth's request to her potential fiancé, *"So spread your covering over your maid..."* As already alluded to, this is the same term used in Ruth 2:12 when Boaz was recounting Ruth's testimony. He spoke of how she had put herself *"under (God's) wings (where) you have come to seek refuge."* What a beautiful word picture! It tells us a lot about Ruth. She had turned (repented) from worshiping created idols in Moab to worshiping the Creator Himself.

Jesus used this same metaphor to describe His relationship with Israel. Listen as He pleads, *"Jerusalem, Jerusalem how many times I would have gathered you under my wings like a hen gathers her chicks, and you would not respond"* (Matthew 23:37 Vinson's paraphrase). Thankfully, Boaz's response to Ruth was much more positive than Jerusalem's response to Jesus.

Listen to Boaz's positive reply: *"Blessed are you of the Lord, my daughter! For you have shown more kindness at the end than at the beginning, in that you did not go after young men, whether poor or rich. And now, my daughter, do not fear. I will do for you all that you request, for all the people of my town know that you are a virtuous woman"* (Ruth 3:10–11 NKJV). In simple language, he said, "Yes!" He was **resolved**, determined that her needs be met, one way or the other.

The obvious question is—why had he not already asked her to be his bride? We have suspected for some time that he really did love her. He couldn't hide his deep respect and affection. But... it was obvious that he was reticent. He seemed to be keenly aware of their age difference. He kept referring to her as "daughter." He also knew that she could marry one of the younger men, should she so choose. Ruth had to take the initiative for him to realize that she was not interested in the younger men. She only had eyes (and heart) for him.

Before we can close this chapter, we must consider one more critical problem that needed resolution before this marriage could be consummated.

Ruth was ready! Boaz was ready! So what was the problem? Here is how Boaz explained the situation to Ruth: "*Now it is true that I am a close relative; however, there is a relative closer than I. Stay this night, and in the morning it shall be that if he will perform the duty of a close relative for you—good; let him do it. But if he does not want to perform the duty for you, then I will perform the duty for you, as the Lord lives! Lie down until morning*" (Ruth 3:12–13).

There was a fly in the ointment, a bump in the road. Boaz explained to Ruth that there was another man more closely related to her than he was. That man had the right of first refusal. If he wouldn't marry Ruth—and Boaz surely hoped he would not—then Boaz certainly would.

We will have to wait until the next chapter to see how this problem was resolved. Don't worry! Rest easy! God was behind the scene and "behind the seen" (meaning Ruth, Boaz and Naomi couldn't observe His activity) working out His perfect will through His good providence. Boaz was worried. Ruth was surprised. But God was neither. None of this caught Him off guard.

Chapter 10

Resting while our Redeemer Works

Wow! What a night. I'm confident Boaz did not get much sleep before he was aroused by the early dawn. He loaded Ruth down with grain and told her to go home and rest. While she relaxed, he would be working out all the details of the kinsman redeemer transaction. Then off to the city gate he went, facing two major objectives: acquiring Elimelech's land for Mahlon's name's sake and acquiring Ruth's hand in marriage for the continuity of Elimelech's family line.

> "Now Boaz went up to the gate and sat down there, and behold, the close relative of whom Boaz spoke was passing by, so he said, 'Turn aside, friend, sit down here.' And he turned aside and sat down. He took ten men of the elders

> *of the city and said, 'Sit down here.' So*
> *they sat down"* (Ruth 4:1).

A mini drama was playing out at the city gate. This was the place where official business was transacted in those days. It was their courthouse, so to speak. If you wanted to find someone this was the place to look. Growing up in Tupelo, Mississippi, I discovered if you hung around the Lee County Court House long enough you could see almost anyone— possibly even Elvis, since Tupelo was his hometown. Today, for chance encounters, Walmart serves the same function. And you don't have to dress up!

Notice Boaz's urgency. Surely he could have waited until he transported his grain to market. But no! His priorities had changed suddenly, literally overnight. Boaz was no longer thinking about his business but about his bride. His focus was not real estate, but Ruth! He could have asked Ruth to move in with him on a trial basis to see if they were compatible; but being the righteous man he was, that was not an option. He did the right thing in the right way.

> *"Then he said to the closest relative,*
> *'Naomi, who has come back from the*
> *land of Moab, has to sell the piece of*
> *land which belonged to our brother*
> *Elimelech. So I thought to inform you,*

> *saying, 'Buy it before those who are sit-*
> *ting here, and before the elders of my*
> *people. If you will redeem it, redeem*
> *it; but if not, tell me that I may know;*
> *for there is no one but you to redeem it,*
> *and I am after you.' And he said, 'I will*
> *redeem it.'"* (Ruth 4:2–4).

The narrator introduces us to the closest redeemer when Boaz approaches him about redeeming Elimelech's land. The man had the right of first refusal to acquire the property. Boaz's heart must have sunk when the unnamed relative responded, "I will redeem it." This response complicated matters. But not to be undone, Boaz had an ace up his sleeve.

> *"Then Boaz said, 'On the day you buy*
> *the field from the hand of Naomi, you*
> *must also acquire Ruth the Moabitess,*
> *the widow of the deceased, in order to*
> *raise up the name of the deceased on*
> *his inheritance'"* (Ruth 4:5).

He changed the focus from Naomi's land to Ruth's hand. He informed the closer kinsman redeemer that whoever exercised the right to redeem the land must also assume the hand of Ruth. It was a "gotcha" moment. Boaz had hooked him and was reeling him in. To the nearer relative it was about land, but to Boaz it was about the lady. Which will win—the land or the lady?

So we have a problem. This stumbling block obviously had not caught God off guard. The Lord behind the seen never has to say, "Oops" or "What shall I do now?" We may have a problem, but be assured, God had a plan. A problem is simply a situation engineered by God, designed to show us the limits of our own resources and to drive us to Himself as our only reasonable alternative.

> *"The closest relative said, 'I cannot redeem it for myself, because I would jeopardize my own inheritance. Redeem it for yourself; you may have my right of redemption, for I cannot redeem it'"* (Ruth 4:6).

Marrying Ruth was not agreeable to the nearer relative. Why? There is no way to be sure, but he may have been too old to father a child for Mahlon. Perhaps he thought he was kinsman redeemer for Naomi, and since she was past childbearing age there would not be a problem. If he married Ruth and she had a son, he would have to divide his inheritance with that son. There is also a good chance he did not want to risk having a Moabite in his family tree, especially in light of what happened to Mahlon and Chilion. To him it just wasn't the logical thing to do. To Boaz assuming the role of kinsman redeemer wasn't about logic but about love.

We are never told who this nearer kinsman is. The narrator seems to be intentionally downplaying the man's significance. He is addressed with a very generic term—friend. *"Turn aside, friend, sit down here"* (Ruth 4:1). It would be similar today to the phrase, "Friend, may I speak with you?" So just who is this nearer kinsman redeemer? He could have been Elimelech's brother by another mother; but truth is, we just do not know. The Hebrew idiom means something like, "Mr. So-and-So, hey pal, hey brother." It is interesting that this man, who was so concerned to preserve his name, never has his name mentioned.

While we do not know who this nearer relative was, we do know that he provides a great illustration of the Mosaic Law. The Law would love to save, just like that nearer relative. In chapter nine we covered the three requirements of a kinsman redeemer. The Law fulfills two of those three requirements. It is <u>related</u> because both are from the Law of God. It comes from a perfect God and therefore is a perfect Law. The Law also has the <u>resolve</u> to save us. All we must do is keep all the Law, all the time. But there is a problem. It comes too late. We have already broken the Law, *"For all have sinned and come short of the glory of God"* (Romans 3:23 KJV).

According to the New Testament book of James, all we must do to be a sinner is to break God's Law one time. *"For whosoever shall keep the whole law (of God), and yet offend in one point, he is guilty of all"* (James 2:10 KJV). The Law is not a cafeteria where we choose the commandment du jour. If we are planning on going to heaven the Law route, it is all or nothing. It is as if we are hanging by a link chain from a helicopter over a volcano. Each link represents one of the Ten Commandments. How many links must break before we fall? Only one! How many commandments must we break to be a law breaker—a sinner? One!

So the Law fails as a means of salvation. The Law is incapable of being our spiritual Kinsman Redeemer, not because of any defect in the Law, but because of our personal defectiveness. The Law was intended to point out our sin, but it has no power to help us overcome sin. In Ruth's story the nearer kinsman, our illustration of the Mosaic Law, said twice in Ruth 4:6, *"... I cannot redeem..., I cannot redeem..."* Paul declared plainly in Galatians 2:21, *"... if righteousness comes through the Law, then Christ died needlessly."*

That is where grace comes in. Boaz is a beautiful picture of the kindness and mercy of God shown through His grace. The Law would have excluded a Moabite widow, even to the tenth generation according to Deuteronomy 23:3. But what the

Law excluded, grace included. As the apostle Paul was to write hundreds of years later, *"But where sin abounded, grace did much more abound"* (Romans 5:20 KJV). The extent of that grace is pervasive. All that Elimelech, Mahlon, and Chilion lost was redeemed by Boaz.

A name missing in Ruth 4 is Orpah. She ought to be there. She started out like she was going to Bethlehem with Naomi and Ruth, but she turned back and went home to Moab. While Boaz was buying the family property, Orpah was sitting in the garbage can called Moab. She could have been in Bethlehem, the House of Bread. The Law said, "Put her out," but God's grace through Boaz said, "Let her in." This made Orpah's return to Moab even more tragic. Boaz's abundant redemptive resources were totally adequate to cover Orpah, but her lack-of-faith decision to return to Moab forever robbed her of that privilege.

> *"Now this was the custom in former times in Israel concerning the redemption and the exchange of land to confirm any matter: a man removed his sandal and gave it to another; and this was the manner of attestation in Israel. So the closest relative said to Boaz, 'Buy it for yourself.' And he removed his sandal"* (Ruth 4:7–8).

Once the decision was made not to serve as Ruth's kinsman redeemer, this unnamed relative took off his sandal and gave it to Boaz. This symbolic act, in essence, became Boaz and Ruth's marriage license. It symbolized the fact that the unnamed relative was giving up his rights to the land and to the lady. Giving the sandal to Boaz was the nearer kinsman's way of saying, "I'm passing on to you the right to walk on Elimelech's property, possess it, and own it." It was a visual way of allowing Bethlehem's elders and the others attending to verify that the transaction had been accomplished.

Just an interesting and significant aside—in those days if a person was refused redemption, they would spit in the face of the nearer kinsman. (Deuteronomy 25:5-10) It was a shameful act not to fulfill the kinsman redeemer responsibility. Consequently, spitting in the face of the refuser was considered the most odious thing a person could do in response to the nearer kinsman's rejection.

Understanding this fact brings new light to what happened when our Lord Jesus was crucified. Mark's gospel repeatedly points out that the Jewish leaders who pronounced Jesus guilty of blasphemy spat in His face. No less than six times the gospels highlight this repulsive act. They were saying, "You did not fulfill your responsibility as our national redeemer."

Since Rome was still in power, the Jews assumed Jesus had failed in His redemptive mission. Only a few days before, they had lined Jerusalem's streets to welcome Jesus in His triumphant entry. Why? Precisely because they thought He was their political messiah. By week's end they considered Him a failure. Even though He had repeatedly told them that His Kingdom was not of this world, they still insisted on a political redeemer. Tragically, the whole time they were spitting in His face, He was dying for their sins. Little did they know that by His crucifixion He was securing their redemption. Isaiah had prophesied Jesus' humiliation, *"I (Jesus) gave my back to the smiters, and my cheeks to them that plucked off the hair: I hid not my face from shame and spitting"* (Isaiah 50:6 KJV).

There is another significant similarity between this Old Testament story and the crucifixion event. The plans for Boaz to redeem Ruth were made in the privacy of Boaz's tent under the Middle Eastern sky. Only Boaz and Ruth were there when the plans were made. But they were paid for publicly at the city gate. And only Boaz said, "I do." Why? Because it was all up to him. He did what the Law could not do. It is the same with our Heavenly Boaz, Jesus Christ. In eternity past, and with perfect harmony, our Triune God made plans for the redemption of the human race. These plans, made in private, included a *"Lamb slain from the foundation of the world"* (Revelation 13:8 KJV). In God's perfect timing these plans were carried out publicly on the cross. In our culture the bride steals the show, but in our spiritual wedding with our Heavenly Boaz, He is the one who receives all the attention.

> "Then Boaz said to the elders and all the people, 'You are witnesses today that I have bought from the hand of Naomi all that belonged to Elimelech and all that belonged to Chilion and Mahlon. Moreover, I have acquired Ruth the Moabitess, the widow of Mahlon, to be my wife in order to raise up the name of the deceased on his inheritance, so that the name of the deceased will not be cut off from his brothers or from the court of his birth place; you are witnesses today.' All the people who were in the court, and the elders, said, 'We are witnesses. May the Lord make the woman who is coming into your home like Rachel and Leah, both of whom built the house of Israel; and may you achieve wealth in Ephrathah and become famous in Bethlehem'" (Ruth 4:9–11).

Boaz openly, publicly, and unashamedly committed his life to Ruth to be her husband, her provider, her protector, and her redeemer. He was not ashamed of the fact that she was a Moabite. How could he be when his own mother was Rahab, also known as "the harlot"? (Matthew 1:5). His Lord and his life had taught him grace and kindness. Jesus was later to say that, *"if we are ashamed of Him and His words, then the Son of Man would be ashamed of us when He comes in His glory"* (paraphrasing Luke 9:26).

The difference between Mr. So-and-So and Boaz can be described with one word: LOVE. Boaz loved Ruth! Consequently, he was willing to sacrifice to have her. He was willing to suffer personal loss if necessary, to have the one he loved. To the nearer relative it didn't seem logical, but to Boaz it wasn't about logic but about love.

So it is with our heavenly Kinsman Redeemer. One thing brought Jesus into the world—LOVE! *"God so loved the world that He gave His only begotten Son..."* (John 3:16 KJV). Hang onto these words: God loves you. Regardless of all that may be going wrong in your life, the cross, the nail prints in His hands, the crown of thorns on His head, all shout from Calvary, "God loves you!"

Marriage is about more than just the emotion of love; it is also about the commitment of love. The marriages I admire are those that have stayed together through thick and thin. The emotion of love will sometimes flicker and grow faint, but the commitment of love is the glue that keeps the marriage together. Emotion likes the "for better" part of the marriage ceremony. Commitment carries us through when "or worse" dominates the circumstances. Ruth and Boaz were not just emotionally involved with warm fuzzy feelings; they were deeply committed to each other and to the covenant of marriage.

Boaz would not rest until he had followed through concerning Ruth's request to be her kinsman redeemer. Similarly, on the seventh day of creation our Lord rested only after completing all that the Father had designed for Him to create. (John 1:3)

May I assure you that you too can rest in your own salvation (Matthew 11:28.) Our Lord Jesus chose not to rest before providing for your salvation. Listen as He cries from the cross, *"It is finished!"* (John 19:30) He did not rest until He had finished the thing He came to do. He was born to die. He was the Lamb *"slain from the foundation of the world"* (Revelation 13:8 KJV). See Him on the cross. Why won't He come down? He could call ten thousand angels to come and rescue Him. He could summon lightening to torch His persecutors. But He didn't! The Man would not abandon the task He came to accomplish. See Him in the grave where He lay until the third day. Watch closely and see Him coming out of the grave on that first Easter Sunday morning—proof positive that He did not rest until He had finished providing for our redemption. Rest in Him and

His finished work, dear reader, for He refused to rest until our redemption was finished.

Chapter 11

Blessed to be a Blessing!

Ruth chapter one began with a famine, three funerals, and crippling failure. Ruth chapter four ends with joy, celebration, singing, and dancing. From weeping to worship is quite a leap. The psalmist captured this wonder when he wrote, *"Weeping may endure for the night, but joy cometh in the morning"* (Psalm 30:5 KJV). Ruth and Naomi *"sow[ed] in tears"* down in Moab, but they *"reap[ed] in joy"* (Psalm 126:5 KJV) when in Bethlehem. It has been inspirational to watch that transition. It offers hope to all of us, regardless of the conditions we are experiencing. Ruth and Naomi were changed from being burdens to being great blessings.

Ruth's example teaches us that the first step toward being a blessing is to humbly "get at the feet" of our Redeemer. Subsequently, opportunities for blessing others are unlimited, provided we do what

He tells us to do. Let's observe a few of the people who were blessed by Ruth.

First and foremost, Ruth was a blessing to Boaz.

> *"Then Boaz said to the elders and all the people, 'You are witnesses today that I have bought from the hand of Naomi all that belonged to Elimelech and all that belonged to Chilion and Mahlon. Moreover, I have acquired Ruth the Moabitess, the widow of Mahlon, to be my wife in order to raise up the name of the deceased on his inheritance, so that the name of the deceased will not be cut off from his brothers or from the court of his birth place; you are witnesses today'"* (Ruth 4:9–10).

Question: What was Boaz like before he married Ruth? Answer: Ruthless! But all that was changing. Look at how their relationship changed over a short period of time. In Ruth chapter one they were strangers. She didn't know Boaz from the proverbial man-in-the-moon. Being a Moabite, she was unfamiliar with most things pertaining to Israel except what she had been able to learn from Naomi. In Ruth chapter two they became acquaintances. She realized she was gleaning in his field and experienced firsthand his grace and kindness. As the chapter concluded she discovered that her boss had more than a casual interest in her. She learned later from Naomi that Boaz was a relative through the family line of her deceased father-in-law and her deceased husband.

By Ruth chapter three things have progressed exponentially. She moved from stranger to fiancé in just two chapters! Engagement took place when Ruth put herself at Boaz's feet. He gladly accepted his responsibility as a kinsman redeemer. From bachelor to boss to her potential bridegroom in approximately two months! To say Ruth was a blessing to Boaz would be an understatement. In Ruth chapter four we witness their marriage. She added value and joy to his life, not to mention becoming the mother of his child.

Has it dawned upon you that, just as Ruth was a blessing to her redeemer, you can also be a blessing to your Redeemer? Often we pray asking to be a blessing to our families and friends. But… have you ever prayed to be a blessing to Jesus our Kinsman Redeemer? We are a part of His bride, and we should be bringing delight to His heart. Can the Lord look at you and say, "This is my beloved child in whom I am well pleased"? Does your life bring joy to Jesus?

Boaz was not the only one blessed by Ruth. Interestingly, this former pagan from the forbidden country of Moab also became a blessing to the whole town of Bethlehem. The very town where the

Messiah would be born (Micah 5:2) was put on the map by this foreigner.

> "All the people who were in the court, and the elders, said, 'We are witnesses. May the Lord make the woman who is coming into your home like Rachel and Leah, both of whom built the house of Israel; and may you achieve wealth in Ephrathah and become famous in Bethlehem. Moreover, may your house be like the house of Perez whom Tamar bore to Judah, through the offspring which the Lord will give you by this young woman'" (Ruth 4:11–12).

So she not only blessed one man, but she was also a blessing to the entire town. When she and Naomi first arrived, they were not much of a blessing to anybody. Naomi especially was not a good neighbor or friend to anyone. She was not pleasant to be around. She was bitter and complained often to the Lord. Now all that has changed.

The people prayed two significant blessings on Ruth and Boaz in Ruth 4:11. First they asked the Lord to bless them with fruitfulness like Rachael and Leah. Those two ladies were prolific in giving birth to what later became Israel. Because Naomi undoubtedly had taught Ruth during their years together about

Israel's history, Ruth could especially identify with the comparison to Rachael. Barren for a great part of her life, she and Mahlon were married for ten years in Moab without conceiving any children. That condition was about to change. The second blessing had to do with their family achieving wealth and fame. Both of these prayers were answered.

Ruth blessed Bethlehem by bearing a child who was to become the grandfather of Israel's great King David. That's not all—in fact it is not even the best part. Through David's line, the Lord Jesus Christ came into the world as the long-expected Messiah. Bethlehem was on the map. Micah's prophesy was fulfilled (Micah 5:2). We would not know much of anything about Bethlehem if it were not for Ruth. As the villagers had prayed, she was made famous in Bethlehem.

Certainly, Ruth was a blessing to her mother-in-law Naomi.

> *"So Boaz took Ruth, and she became his wife, and he went in to her. And the Lord enabled her to conceive, and she gave birth to a son. Then the women said to Naomi, 'Blessed is the Lord who has not left you without a redeemer today, and may his name become famous in Israel. May he also be to you a restorer of life and a sustainer of your old age; for your*

133

> *daughter-in-law, who loves you and is*
> *better to you than seven sons, has given*
> *birth to him'"* (Ruth 4:13–15).

Actually she had already proven herself to be invaluable to Naomi in many ways. Her mother-in-law's emptiness has now changed to fullness. Her sadness has turned into joyfulness. Real hope has replaced her hopelessness. I hate to think what might have happened to Naomi if Ruth had opted to return to Moab like her sister-in-law Orpah. For that matter, I hate to think of what might have happened to you and me. Can you imagine a world with no Jesus? No Messiah. No Savior. No Hope. Only a sovereign God, who can do exceedingly, abundantly above all that we could ask or think (Eph. 3:20), could hang the hopes of the world on the conception of a baby in the womb of a childless widow of ten years, and the baby's father is past middle age.

Even though Elimelech had been dead for over ten years, Ruth became a great blessing to him as well. She was the human instrument God used to keep his family name alive. For a Jewish family, this continuance was of paramount importance.

> *"Then Naomi took the child and laid*
> *him in her lap, and became his nurse"*
> (Ruth 4:16).

Now, instead of Elimelech's widow being empty-handed, she is holding his grandson. The people viewed him almost as if he was Naomi's child. What a blessing! Now she was learning what many of us have come to realize: grandchildren are really grand!

Let us learn this lesson well: when we place ourselves at the feet of our Redeemer, He can then use us to be a blessing to others in a myriad of ways. Warren Wiersbe points out that Naomi now had a full heart, full home, full arms, and full hands. She was a blessed woman. (Wiersbe, Warren. *Put Life Together, p.* 94)

We have seen only a microcosm of those who were genuinely blessed by this extraordinary woman Ruth. She was in fact a blessing to all of Israel. The baby she delivered was destined to become the grandfather of King David who elevated the status of the entire nation of Israel. *"The neighbor women gave him a name,* saying, *'A son has been born to Naomi!' So they named him Obed. He is the father of Jesse, the father of David"* (Ruth 4: 17). The name Obed means "servant" and is probably an abbreviated form of Obadiah which means "servant of the Lord."

Chronologically Ruth 1:1-5 covers about ten years; Ruth 1:6 through 4:12 covers at most a few months; then 4:13 summarizes the better part of a year. Although the writer acknowledged the wonder of the new marriage, his primary concern was with the child it produced. In fact, this family's genealogy seems to be one of the primary reasons Ruth's little four-chapter book is included in the Bible. It can only be attributed to God's grace that an idol-worshiping woman from Moab could find herself in Israel's royal family tree.

Think about it—Boaz and Ruth's son Obed became the grandfather of David, the greatest King in Israel's history. I can't imagine a Bible without David. As a poet he wrote many of the Psalms. As a musician he calmed the demon-possessed Saul. As a shepherd he killed a lion and a bear. As a military genius he led a powerful army. As a sovereign king He was used of God to prepare for the temple's construction. He brought the nation together and made her great. And it all happened because of what God did in making Ruth a blessing to Israel.

Finally and ultimately, Ruth became a blessing to the whole world. Through her book the world can learn so much about our sovereign God. When she lay down at the feet of her kinsman redeemer, she had no idea how famous her name would become throughout the world. Ruth, the grandmother of King David, is well known among people of Biblical faith. It could be said of her what Jesus said of Mary of Bethany, *"What this woman has done will be spoken of in memory of her"* (Mark 14:9).

Consider Ruth's genealogy as recorded in the New Testament's gospel of Matthew, and we get a wonderful glimpse into the gracious nature of the

God of the Bible. Matthew names one prostitute, one daughter-in-law who deceived her father-in-law into having sex with her, one adulteress, and one idolater (Matthew 1:3–6) in the family tree of the Lord Jesus Christ. Tamar (deceiving daughter-in-law), Rahab (prostitute), Ruth (idolater), and Bathsheba (adulteress) were not candidates to teach the ladies' Bible class! All four of these flawed women were gentiles. Their inclusion in this lineage points to the fact that the gospel is for all people. If God can use someone like this quartet of ladies to accomplish His divine purposes, then we have reason to hope. One of the early converts in a Billy Graham crusade was a Los Angeles disc jockey named Stuart Hamblen. After he was saved, he wrote the popular gospel song *It Is No Secret.* He captured this truth with the lyrics, "It is no secret what God can do. What He's done for others, He'll do for you. With arms wide open He'll pardon you. It is no secret what God can do."

That Ruth was a blessing to the whole world is primarily because of David. Why? Because it was through David's family line that God chose to bring His Son Jesus Christ to the earth. Repeatedly He is referred to in the New Testament as Jesus Christ, the *"Son of David"*. Listen as a woman from the gentile territory of Canaan cries out, *"Have mercy on me, O Lord, Son of David!"* (Matt. 15:22) Two blind men from Jericho called to him, *"Have mercy on us, O Lord, Son of David!"* (Matt. 20:30) Isaiah the prophet proclaimed that one day Christ would sit on the *"throne of David* (Isaiah 9:6–7). Therefore, more than ever before, we can say that Ruth was a blessing to the world.

Remember how at the beginning of Ruth's book everything was falling apart? How encouraging it is to note that by the end of it, God put things back together again. This example reassures me that God can put our lives back together also. Ruth's book ends on a happy note. Ruth is like the little boy at the pet shop who said, "I want the puppy with a happy ending."

Do you want to be a genuine blessing to other people? Then put yourself at the feet of Him who has the right to redeem you. This can be none other than the Lord Jesus Christ. As your Kinsman Redeemer He is related to you in that He shares your humanity. He is willing to redeem you, for He says, *"[I am] not willing that any should perish, but that all should come to repentance"* (2 Peter 3:9 KJV). Regardless of your past, your pedigree, or your performance, He is able to forgive your sins and make you His child. In fact the Bible says *that, "He is able also to save them to the uttermost that come unto God by Him"* (Hebrews 7:25 KJV). Then you can be a blessing to others.

You can be a blessing:

- To your God by loving and obeying Him.

- To your family by loving and leading them in the ways of Christ.
- To your church by your prayers and faithful service.
- To our broken world by listening to people's hurts, loving them unconditionally, and sharing the message of hope through the gospel of our Lord Jesus Christ.

I began this book by referring to a series of messages on Ruth which I heard fifty years ago from British Bible teacher Major Ian Thomas. Let me close by sharing something else he taught me that week. He concluded his last message by asking the congregation to turn to Ruth chapter five. We quickly discovered that such a chapter did not exist. The Major then used his prolific imagination to envision a chapter five. "Suppose," he said, "that Ruth decided one day that she needed to go back out to the barley fields and grub up some food for breakfast. Boaz hears her stirring, sees her leaving, and rushes to the door to say to her, 'Ruth, where are you going?' She responds that she is going into the fields to glean a bit of food so they can eat. Boaz is bewildered! He replies, 'Ruth, don't you know that everything I have belongs to you? Your grubbing days are over. You are my wife. What is mine is yours. There are abundant resources sufficient to meet every need you have.

All you have to do is ask." (Thomas, final sermon in series on Ruth.)

What was true of Ruth and her kinsman redeemer is also true of every follower of Jesus Christ. Listen to this precious promise: *"But my God shall supply all your need according to His riches in glory by Christ Jesus"* (Philippians 4:19 KJV). The enemy will promise you anything to get you to turn your back on Jesus. Don't listen to his lies. It is not worth it. He always has more in the show window than he has in the warehouse. Jesus is enough!

This Bible book that begins in Bethlehem and ends with the birth of a baby has won my heart. I hope that it has blessed yours. Fifty-six years ago (as I write this), I humbled my prideful heart, got at the feet of Him who has the right to redeem, surrendered my sinful heart to Jesus Christ, and by faith embraced the gospel. I could not have imagined where that decision would take me.

Poet Lorrie Cline captured well the heart of my testimony when she wrote...

I Met the Master Face to Face.
I had walked life's way with an easy tread,
Had followed where comforts and pleasures led,
Until one day in a quiet place,
I met the Master face to face.

I met Him and knew Him, and blushed to see,

That His eyes full of sorrow were fixed on me;
And I faltered and fell at His feet that day,
While my castles all melted, vanished away.

Melted and vanished, and in their place,
Naught else did I see but the Master's face.
And I cried aloud, "Lord, make me meek,
To follow the steps of Thy wounded feet."

My thought is now for the souls of men.
I have lost my life to find it again,
E'er since one day in a quiet place,
I met the Master face to face.

BIBLIOGRAPHY

1. Anders, Max and GaryW. Phillips. *Holman Old Testament Commentary, Judges and Ruth.* Nashville, TN: Holman Publishers, 2004.

2. Atkinson, David. *The Message of Ruth,* Downer's Grove, Illinois: InterVarsity Press, 1985.

3. Block, Daniel. *New American Commentary, Judges and Ruth.* Nashville, TN; Broadman Holman Publishers,1999.

4. DeHaan, M.R. *The Romance of Redemption.* Grand Rapids, MI: Zondervan, 1958.

5. Dunn, Ronn. *God's Test* sermon. Crossgates Baptist Church, Brandon, MS: 1991.

6. Hanford, Jack, and Dick Eastman. *31 Days Meditating on the Majesty of Jesus.* Dario Stream, IL: Tyndall House Publishing, 2007.

7. Hawkins, O.S. *Tracing the Rainbow Through the Rain.* Nashville, TN: Broadway Press, 1985.

8. Luter, Boyd A. and Barry C. Davis. *Ruth and Esther, God Behind the Seen.* Grand Rapids, MI: Baker Book House, 1995.

9. McGee, J. Vernon. *Ruth.* Glendale, CA: Through the Bible Books, 1980.

10. Miller, Paul E. *A Loving Life.* Wheaton, IL: Crossway, 2014.

11. Phillips, John. *Exploring People f the Old Testament, Volume Two.* Grand Rapids, MI: Kregel Publishing, 2006.

12. Piper, John. Sermon series on Ruth. Bethlehem Baptist Church, Minneapolis, MN.

13. Platt, David. Sermon series on Ruth preached in The Church at Brook Hills, Birmingham, Al.

14. Thomas, Major Ian. Sermon series through Ruth preached in ARP Presbyterian Church, New Albany, MS: 1970.

15. Tozer, A.W. *Knowledge of the Holy.* Lincoln, NE: Back to the Bible, 1971.

16. Walvoord, John and Roy Zuck. *Bible Knowledge Commentary, Old Testament.* USA, Canada, England: Victor Books, 1983.

17. Wiersbe, Warren. *Be Committed.* Colorado Springs, CO: Victor Books, 1996.

18. Wiersbe, Warren. *Put Your Life Together.* Wheaton, IL: Victor Books, 1985.

9 781662 810862